PROCESSING COMMUNICATION

PROCESSING COMMUNICATION

Information Processing in Intrapersonal Communication

Blaine Goss
University of Oklahoma

Wadsworth Publishing Company
Belmont, California
A Division of Wadsworth, Inc.

Speech Communications Editor: Kevin Howat
Production Editor: Donna Oberholtzer
Designer: Adriane Bosworth
Copy Editor: Dott Morrissey
Technical Illustrators: Lisa L. Palacio, Alan Noyes, Lois Stanfield

Printed in the United States of America
1 2 3 4 5 6 7 8 9 10—86 85 84 83 82

Library of Congress Cataloging in Publication Data

Goss, Blaine.
   Processing communication.

   Bibliography: p.
   Includes index.
   1. Interpersonal communication. 2. Communication—Psychological aspects. I. Title.
HM132.G67   302.2   81-11621
ISBN 0-534-01010-5   AACR2

CONTENTS

PREFACE   ix

PART 1: SOME BASICS   1

Chapter 1: Perceiving Information   3
A Model   3
External and Internal Information   5
Boulding's Image   5
Perception   6
    Closure   6   Familiarity   7   Expectations   7
    Process and Products   8   Selectivity   8
    Review   10
Summary   10
Summary Propositions   10

Chapter 2: Necessary Equipment   13
The Brain   13
    Cerebral Cortex   14   Cerebral Lateralization   15
The Ears and Eyes   16
    Principles of Sensation   16   Hearing and Vision   16
    Coordinated Inputs   17
Some Assumptions   18
    Active Processing   18   Structuring Information   18
    Orderliness   19
Summary   19
Summary Propositions   19

PART 2: HUMAN INFORMATION PROCESSING   21

Chapter 3: Gathering Information   23
What Is Information?   23
    Defining Information   23
    Quantity and Quality of Information   24
    Noise   24   Summary   24
Sensation   24
    Signals   25   Pattern Recognition   25

Attention   25
   Three Principles   *26*   *Information/Noise Ratio*   *26*
   Managing I/N   *27*   *Depth of Processing*   *28*
Perception   29
   Selective Perception   *29*
Summary   30
Summary Propositions   30

Chapter 4: Storing and Retrieving Information   33
Short-term Memory   33
   Duration   *33*   *Rehearsal*   *33*   *Chunking*   *34*
   Forgetting   *34*
Long-term Memory   35
   Accessibility   *35*   *Organization*   *36*
   Forgetting   *36*
STM and LTM Compared   37
Successful Storage   38
Recalling Information   38
Kinds of Remembering   39
   Recognition   *39*   *Cued Recall*   *39*
   Noncued Recall   *39*
Message Distortions   40
   Primacy-Recency   *40*
   Leveling, Sharpening, and Assimilation   *40*
Summary   41
Summary Propositions   41

Part 3: COGNITIVE COMPONENT   43

Chapter 5: Meaning   45
What Is Meaning?   45
   Formal Level   *46*   *Functional Level*   *46*
   Affective Level   *46*   *Combining the Levels*   *47*
Organization of Meaning   47
   Semantic Memory   *47*   *Meanings as Categories*   *48*
   Verbal Associations   *48*   *Learning Associations*   *49*
   Meanings and Natural Language Usage   *49*
   Summary   *50*
Forms of Meaning   50
Creating Meaning   51
Summary   52
Summary Propositions   52

Chapter 6: Language   55
Centrality of Language   55
   Language Competence and Performance   *56*
Competence and Communication   57

Nonverbal Information   57
   Paralanguage and Kinesics   58
   Nonverbal Memory   58   Imagery   58
Language Learning   59
   Hypothesis Testing   59   Language Universals   60
   Four Principles of Language Learning   60
   Language Learning and HIP   61
Summary   62
Summary Propositions   62

PART 4: AFFECTIVE COMPONENT   65

Chapter 7: Attitudes and Self-Concept   67
Consistency   67
   Striving for Consistency   68   Psycho-Logic   68
VAB System   69
   Values   69   Attitudes   70   Beliefs   70
Self-Concept   71
   Learning Your Self-Concept   72
   Low Self-Concept   72   Cognitive Complexity   73
   Some Risks   74
Summary   74
Summary Propositions   75

Chapter 8: Consistency Theories   77
Balance   77
   P−O−X Triangles   77   Preference for Balance   79
   Unit Relationship   79   Timing   80
Congruity   80
   Applications to HIP   81
Cognitive Dissonance   82
   Justification   82   Postdecisional Dissonance   83
   Selective Exposure   83
   Resolving Inconsistency   84   Applications to HIP   84
Summary   85
Summary Propositions   85

PART 5: OPERATIONAL COMPONENT   87

Chapter 9: Listening   89
Encoding and Decoding   89
Hearing versus Listening   90
Selectivity in Listening   90
Requirements for Listening   91
   Speech Recognition   91
   Readiness to Respond   92
   Meaningful Response   92

Listening Comprehension 92
   Innate Speech Processor *93*
   Listening Strategies *93*
   Listening Compared with Reading *94*
   Dual Coding and Rambling Recall *95*
Improving Listening 95
   Step One *95*   *Step Two* *96*
Summary 96
Summary Propositions 97

Chapter 10: Speaking   **99**
Spontaneous Speech 99
   Interface of Language, Speech, and Meaning *99*
   Planning and Monitoring *100*   *Summary* *100*
Natural Speech Output 101
   Length of Utterances *101*   *Speech Errors* *101*
   Speaking Rate *101*   *Vocabulary* *101*
   Nonfluencies *102*   *Pausing* *102*
   Summary *103*
Paraphrasing 103
   Creating Sentences *104*
Schemata 105
   Using Schemata *105*   *Schemata and Themes* *105*
   Schemata and Conversation *106*
   Making Inferences *106*
   Logical and Pragmatic Implications *107*
Summary 108
Summary Propositions 108

EPILOGUE   **111**

APPENDIX: TAKING NOTES AND STUDYING FOR EXAMS   **113**

REFERENCES   **115**

GLOSSARY   **121**

INDEX   **127**

PREFACE

I think that you are going to like this book. It is about you and your basic abilities to handle communication. As I wrote it, I saw many things about me in it. As you read it, you should see yourself in it as well.

I wrote this book because many communication courses pay only passing attention to the intrapersonal aspects of human communication. These fundamental processes are crucial to all levels of communication. Consequently, this book is written for the student who wants to know more about his or her individual ability to process communication. This book, then, would have many applications in a number of different courses.

For many people, intrapersonal communication is a difficult area of study. But as you read this text, you will soon realize that the material is quite understandable. In ten chapters, I have drawn ideas from a number of sources that help us realize the nature of intrapersonal communication. This book represents my attempt to show how research in the cognitive aspects of human beings can be applied to communication. The first two chapters lay the groundwork and present my model of intrapersonal communication. The following chapters explore the major components of the model. They are best read in pairs, since each part of my model requires two chapters. For instance, human information processing is covered in Chapters 3 and 4. The three surrounding components (cognitive, affective, and operational) are dealt with in Chapters 5 and 6; 7 and 8; and 9 and 10.

In essence, this book is not a research text. It is not loaded with endless references and filled with complicated jargon. Rather it is written for the undergraduate student who wishes to learn more about his or her communication abilities. For the reader who finds unfamiliar terms in the text, I have included a glossary at the end of the book.

This book, like others, is a joint effort. I wrote it, but my reviewers made outstanding recommendations for improvement. For those comments, I want to thank John Petelle of the University of Nebraska; Mark Milkovich of the University of Utah; Patrick Garner of Harding College; William Powers of North Texas State University; Diane Atkinson Gorcyca of Iowa State University; Ken Frandsen of the University of New Mexico; and Thomas Housel of the University of Kentucky.

Without the insight and encouragement of my editor at Wadsworth, Curt Peoples, this book might still be in folders in my filing cabinet. He is a good editor. Another person at Wadsworth deserves special mention. Henry Staat did more than anyone else to see that the original manuscript would be well received by the publisher. He spoke favorably of the manuscript and spoke favorably of me as well. His judgment on the first matter is well founded. I am not always sure of the second issue.

Finally, let me acknowledge the production staff who helped develop the book itself. The quality of their work is evident.

Lastly, I must acknowledge my wife, Carol, and two sweet daughters, Angela and Melissa, who willingly took a long vacation to Grandma's so that I could write this book in one major sitting. I missed them, but I finished the book.

1 SOME BASICS

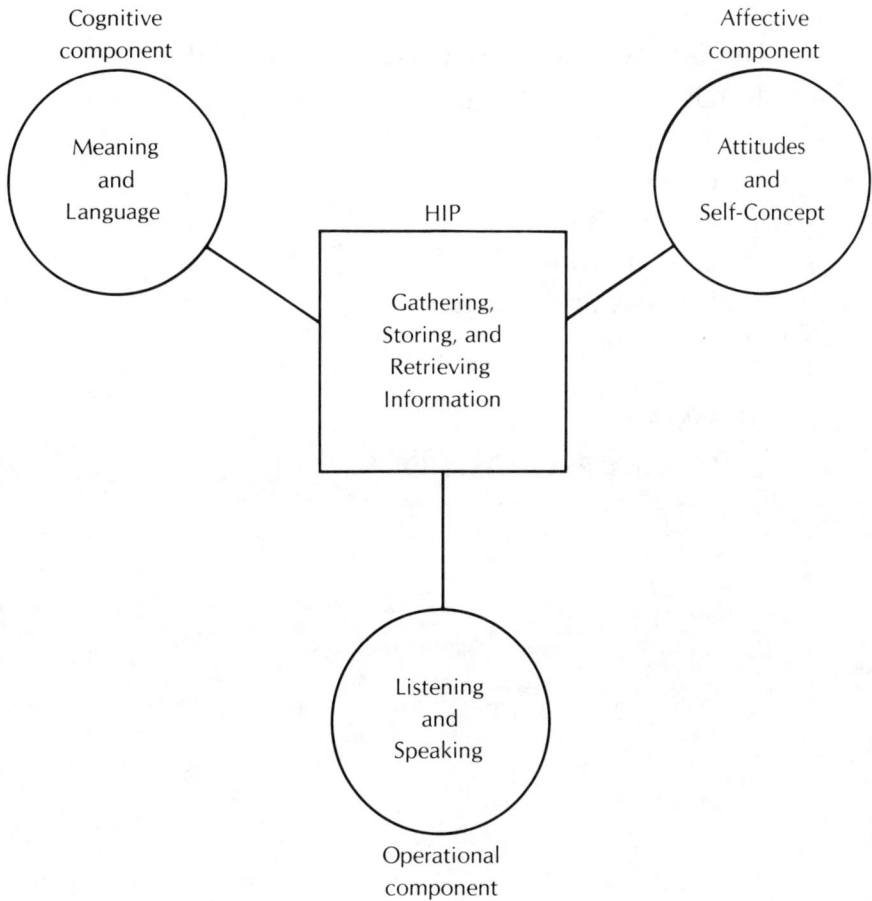

Chapter 1

A MODEL
EXTERNAL AND INTERNAL INFORMATION
BOULDING'S IMAGE
PERCEPTION
    Closure
    Familiarity
    Expectations
    Process and Products
    Selectivity
    Review
SUMMARY
SUMMARY PROPOSITIONS

Perceiving Information

Because you use communication skills every day, you don't think about them very much. The ability to talk and listen seems to come naturally. Consequently, your communication skills are easy to take for granted. But when you take these skills for granted, you often lose sight of the very basic processes that make it possible for you to communicate in the first place. Communication doesn't just happen. You make it happen. You must possess certain skills in order to say anything—to say your name, to ask for information, or to arrange a date for the weekend. For instance, do you know how your memory makes it possible for you to participate in everyday conversations? Do you understand how your ears and eyes determine what information you hear and see? Do you know which mental skills are necessary for you to speak? These and many other questions can be answered when you understand the intrapersonal processes of communication. That is what this book is about.

You are reading a book about your own abilities to produce and comprehend communication. It is centered on something called *human information processing*. Together we will see how your abilities to process information allow you to communicate. As we proceed, you will notice that as a processor of information you are not just a computer. Computers are without emotion, whereas your emotions, attitudes, and feelings contribute heavily to how you react to information. Additionally, computers do not have self-concepts—they don't even "know" they exist. You do, and it makes a big difference. Most importantly, computers cannot initiate communication. You can. You don't need to be plugged in to behave. You are behaving all the time.

What all this means is that as a communicator, you are a multifaceted person. When you speak, write, listen, or read, you engage many of your mental abilities to help you understand what is going on. For instance, if someone asks you an apparently simple question such as, "Where were you born?", your answer will be a function of what you heard (hearing), how you interpret it (listening, perception), how you feel about it (attitudes), and what you know about it (memory). Your answer will also be governed by your encoding skills (speaking and writing). You see, being a competent communicator means that you can call up what you *know* and how you *feel* in order to send, receive, and store information. And all these combined make up your intrapersonal processes for communication.

A MODEL

To begin to understand intrapersonal communication, let's start with a model of its processes. Please notice that I am talking about *intra*personal processes, and not *inter*personal aspects. The term *intra*personal refers to processes *within* the person. On the other hand, *inter*personal refers to things going on between people. This model illustrates the fundamental processes within the person that allow communication to take place. As Figure 1.1 illustrates, the center of the system is human information

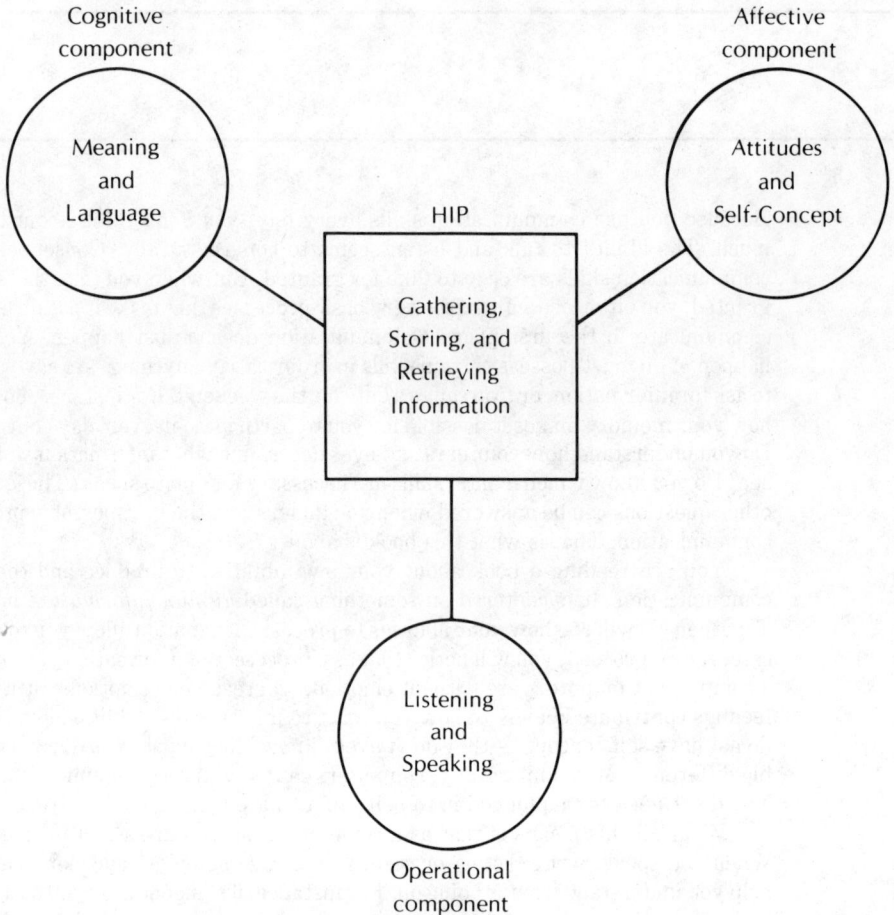

Figure 1.1   The components of the intrapersonal processes of communication.

processing (HIP). *Human information processing is the ability to gather, store, and retrieve information.* This is the crux of intrapersonal communication. Surrounding HIP are three components, each with two parts. The *cognitive* component consists of your meaning and language. The *affective* component consists of your attitudes and self-concept. Finally, the third component, called the *operational* component, refers to your listening and speaking skills. All three components have a strong influence on basic HIP. It is important to understand that HIP is the center of this model, but the other three components contribute to the intrapersonal processes of communication.

This book is organized around this model. The first two chapters lay the groundwork for a closer inspection of HIP, which follows in Chapters 3 and 4. Chapters 5 and 6 demonstrate how meaning and language (cognitive component) affect HIP. Chapters 7 and 8 cover the affective component of the model. Finally, Chapters 9 and 10 reveal how HIP is evident in listening and speaking (operational component). Key terms used throughout the text are included in the Glossary. When you finish reading this book you should have a good understanding of the intrapersonal processes that make communication possible for you. For now, let's begin to explore how you process information.

EXTERNAL AND INTERNAL INFORMATION

The information that you cope with daily has two origins. Some of it is *external* information; the rest of it is *internal* information. People, events, and objects are sources for external information. Knowledge, past experiences, meanings, and feelings make up your internal world of information. Successful information processing depends on the merger of external and internal information. Rarely, if ever, do you process information with only one of the two sources. How you receive, retrieve, and send information is grounded in the combining of what you are now experiencing (external) with what you know and feel (internal). For instance, this text is a source of external information, but you must have a sufficient understanding of my words and ideas inside your head before I can say that I have communicated. Without your internal information (knowledge and feelings), this source of external information might go unnoticed. As Miller (1968) notes, "most scientifically useful generalizations concerning human information processing will have to take account of both the environmental stimuli available to the individual . . . and the background of experiences that he brings to the situation . . ." (p. 53). In a later chapter, I will consider more closely and precisely what constitutes information. For now, let's look at how a well-known social scientist views information.

BOULDING'S IMAGE

In 1956, Kenneth Boulding wrote a delightful book describing the essence of knowledge, which he called an *image* of the world. According to Boulding, you have developed, over your lifetime, personally ordered images of the world. You know, to some degree, who you are, where you are, and when you are. In other words, you have located yourself in time and space. You also have images of other people, events, and objects in your world. Any image that you have, however, does not always remain the same. An image can be changed by new information about it. New experiences and new information have one of four effects on your image: (1) they can add information to your image, (2) they can reinforce your present image, (3) they can produce a slight alteration in your image, or (4) they can force a thorough restructuring of your image. Furthermore, your images affect how receptive you will be to new information. Information and images go together.

The important thing to notice about Boulding's images is that they are outgrowths of the interaction of external information with internal information. Furthermore, images are not unchanging. Each new experience (external information) has the potential to alter your images (internal information). For example, your self-concept may change as a function of being praised for a good job. If someone says that you did a "fine job on that project," and if that person is important to you, the compliment can boost your self-concept. As another example, suppose you raise show dogs. After many months of preparation, you bring your favorite dog to a statewide show. You might have an uncertain image of your dog because it has never been "shown" before, but in your mind this is a fine dog. If you win a ribbon with your dog, your positive image will be reinforced. If, however, you are not awarded a ribbon, you might have to alter your image of your canine. The more that external and internal information have a chance to interact, the more likely your images will be affected.

Something else is important here. Images, once formed, become filters. In other words, how you interpret your external world is strongly influenced by your internal images. You use your internal images as filters through which you can view reality. These filters develop over time. As you grow older, experience more, and understand more about yourself, you build a personal storehouse of knowledge about yourself and your world. Moreover, you must personally construct your images of the world. Knowledge is not handed to you "on a platter." You must work it out for yourself.

PERCEPTION

Whenever you encounter information, you must make some immediate decisions about its meaning. As Smith (1975) says, you must make sense out of it. Whereas you are "wired" for sensation (eyes, ears, etc.), you must learn to perceive. You must organize your sensations (bits of information sent by the sensory organs) to create "wholes" that you recognize. This process of organizing is called *perception*. It is the first stage of assigning meaning. It is making sense out of a barrage of inputs.

For purposes of economy, most people perceive in ways to make things simple and orderly. In other words, to reduce the confusion of all the inputs from the eyes and ears, you find ways to structure the incoming information into its simplest and most orderly form. In doing so, you demonstrate two common perceptual tendencies: closure and familiarity.

Closure

Closure means that you see things as complete wholes rather than as incomplete configurations. With the smallest amount of data, you make major inferences about the whole. The figures below illustrate the point:

Most people see the figures as a triangle and a circle. Yet neither is presented in its complete form. *You* do the completing. Hence, closure is completing an incomplete figure, thought, or idea.

Familiarity

Familiarity suggests that you identify input as representatives of things you already know. In other words, you recognize familiar things more readily than unfamiliar things, and you are more likely to see the familiar aspects of something than the unfamiliar aspects.

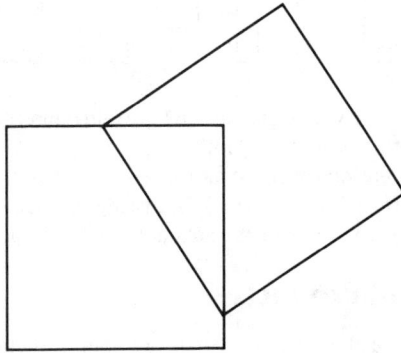

In the figure above, what do you see? Two overlapping squares? Could there be three figures, all irregular in shape? Since you are more familiar with squares than you are with irregular shapes, you "see" two squares. Thus, your perceptions tend toward the familiar. You look for the normal rather than the unusual.

Expectations

To take this analysis of perception a step farther, you should realize that perception is a matter of expectations. You see what you expect to see. You hear what you want to hear. Perception is a very subjective process.

The more often you perceive something, the more "fixed" in your mind becomes your perception of it. Over time, your perceptions become habits. These habits make it difficult to analyze objectively such tasks as:

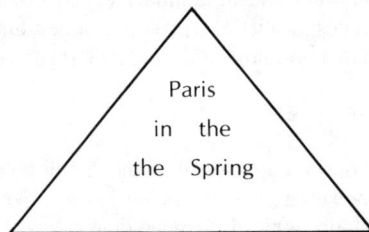

Paris
in   the
the   Spring

What do you see here? Did you read this as "Paris in the Spring"? Did you notice the duplication of "the"? Many people don't. The reason is that you probably know the expression and therefore ignore the improper grammar. If you have never heard the expression, you might more readily notice the grammatical error.

What do you see here?

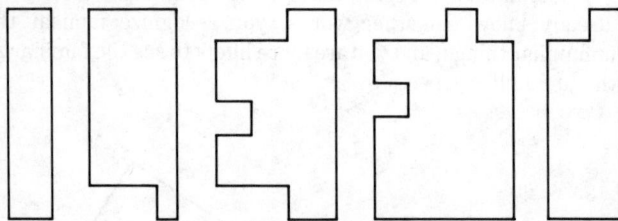

Depending on how you organize the figure-ground relationship of the illustration, you will or will not see the word "left."

Your perceptions of these figures were probably not based solely on the figures as presented (external information), but rather on what was presented *and* on what you expected to see. Your expectations determine, in part, your perceptions.

Process and Products

By now you should be aware of two things about perception. One is that perception is both a process and a product. By process I mean that perception is a way of forming recognizable wholes from what you see and hear. The process of perceiving is a psychological phenomenon; it is the manner in which you interpret your sensations. You can use the word "perception" in the same way you can use a word such as "building." In construction, building is something that you do. Likewise, you build a building. Building, then, can refer to the process of building or to the end product itself (a building). Perception, too, can be a process or a product. The products of perception, or *percepts*, represent what you think you experienced. These percepts are stored in memory and saved to enable you to understand future events.

The other thing you should realize about the process and products of perception is that they are learned. Your past experience has left you with a number of percepts (products). The way that you remember these percepts is a function of how they were learned (process). For instance, if you had difficulty with the illustrations used in this section, it was probably caused by the various percepts you learned earlier in life. You may have read "Paris in the Spring" instead of "Paris in the the Spring." (Did I catch you again?)

The notions of closure, familiarity, and expectations remind us how the process of perception leaves us with the products of perception. And you now know that perceptions are learned and stored in memory for future use.

Selectivity

As you continue in this text, more will be said about the perceptual processes. Right now, however, you might be asking "So what?" If everyone perceives in the foregoing fashion, what difference does it make to communication?

To answer these questions, let us contemplate two propositions: (1) *How you perceive things determines what you attend to (what information you are susceptible to).* I remember going to a local pizza parlor not too long ago, placing my order, and patiently waiting for my number to be called, indicating my pizza was ready. After listening attentively for number 28 (my number) and then eating my pizza, I noticed that the next number I heard was 39! Surely pizza number 39 was not the next one after mine to be ready for pickup. What obviously happened was that given no further need to monitor the loudspeaker, I didn't listen again until I was sufficiently satisfied by my meal. Hence, I was not a very receptive listener to the intervening messages. How often do you find yourself ignoring messages that don't seem immediately relevant?

This is called *selective attention*. It is the act of filtering out only that information that seems important at the time. What determines what you selectively attend to? Well, let's backtrack a bit. How you perceive things determines what you look for. Right now, for instance, can you tell me the color of the eyes of the person you last talked with? For many of us, that would be hard to do, because we do not necessarily watch people's eyes. And when we do, we don't often notice the color of the eyes. Why not? An optician would. Why wouldn't you? It all depends on how important you perceive eye color to be in order to understand something about that person. In many ways, your selective attention depends on your training. If you have been trained to notice the color of people's eyes, you will. Now, to the next proposition.

(2) *Your perceptions affect how you recall information at a later time.* This is known as *selective recall*. Selective recall occurs when you try to piece together a prior event based on your memory. Sometimes what is stored is incomplete. Other times, your recall is selective because you are trying to make sense out of an item being recalled. In other words, if I asked you to describe your bedroom when you were ten years old, you would piece together a description that would not always be well organized, and furthermore, you would forget to include some details in your description. That is selective recall.

An interesting study of selective recall occurred when Carmichael, Hogan, and Walter (1932) exposed subjects to a number of drawings similar to the following:

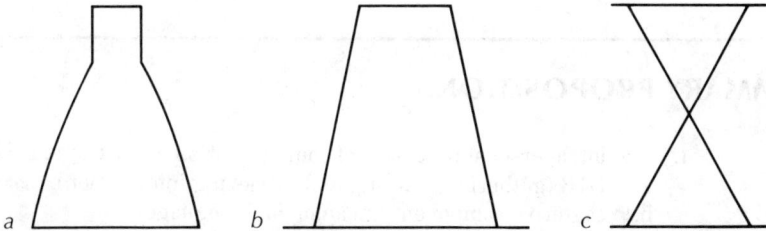

The subjects were told that the figures were drawings of simple concepts. Half the people were told that each drawing represented a certain concept, while the other half were told that the drawing represented a different concept. For instance, half were told that figure *a* was a *bottle*; the others were told it was a *stirrup*. For figure *b*, half were told it was a *beehive*; the other half, a *hat*. For figure *c*, half were told it was an *hourglass*, and the others that it was a *table*.

When asked at a later time to draw the figures they saw, the subjects modified them to correspond closely to the associated label that they learned with the figure. Most people fit their drawings to the words rather than to the original drawings. Consequently, figure *a* was altered to look more like either a stirrup or a bottle, depending on which group the subject was in. Figure *b* was drawn to look more like either a beehive or a hat, and figure *c* was recreated to look more like either an hourglass or a table. The *concept*, not the original stimulus, dominated their recall.

Had the people not been given labels for these figures, they would have produced drawings that more closely fit the original drawings. But because they had in their minds that the figures were to represent a concept, they "corrected" each figure to look more like the concept. This kind of correction in memory is common. When recalling any past event, you often "repair it" so that the recalled version is perhaps more perfect that the original. This is selective recall.

Review

Perception is the process of organizing your sensations into recognizable wholes. It is the first step in assigning meaning. Perception is both a process and a product. The products of perception (percepts) are learned and stored for future use. Your prior experience produces expectations that cause you to see or hear what you expect to see or hear. Although your expectations may not allow you to perceive an event correctly, your expectations are usually accurate and thus they are useful to you. Finally, selective perceptions can lead to selective attention and selective recall.

SUMMARY

The key to human information processing resides in perception. Whenever you produce and comprehend communication, you use your perceptual skills. As Neisser (1976) concludes, ". . . perceiving is the basic cognitive activity out of which all others emerge . . ." (p. 9). If Neisser is correct, and I think he is, then perceiving is processing, and processing is perceiving. Perceiving information is what the intrapersonal processes of communication are all about.

SUMMARY PROPOSITIONS

1. The intrapersonal processes of communication consist of four major parts:
    a. HIP (gathering, storing, and retrieving information).
    b. cognitive component (meaning and language).
    c. affective component (attitudes and self-concept).
    d. operational component (listening and speaking).
2. We have two sources of information—external and internal.
3. We form images and perceptions based on the interaction of external information with internal information.
4. We must learn to perceive.
5. Our perceptions, as products, can be used as filters for future inputs.
6. Selective perception leads to selective attention and selective recall.

Chapter 2

THE BRAIN
    Cerebral Cortex
    Cerebral Lateralization
THE EARS AND EYES
    Principles of Sensation
    Hearing and Vision
    Coordinated Inputs
SOME ASSUMPTIONS
    Active Processing
    Structuring Information
    Orderliness
SUMMARY
SUMMARY PROPOSITIONS

Necessary Equipment

In Chapter 1 you saw how HIP, in general, works. You saw that it is dependent on the process of perception. Before exploring the psychological aspects of HIP in more detail, you need to step back and reflect on the very basic physiological equipment that makes gathering, storing, and retrieving information possible. You need to know about you in a physical sense so you can understand what you can and cannot do. The very nature of your ears and eyes and brain often determines *what* information you process and *how* you can handle that information. If people were constructed differently than they are, researchers would have to develop a different theory of information processing. Any theory about information processing must operate within the physiological boundaries of the subjects being studied. Researchers were reminded of this when a number of them set out to teach chimpanzees to talk. Unfortunately, they forgot to consult a physiologist, who could have told them that chimps will never talk because they do not have the proper vocal apparatus in their throats to produce sounds like humans. Consequently, many hours were spent trying to teach animals to do something that was physically impossible for them to do!

Fortunately, you have been given the necessary equipment for HIP. Not only can you talk, you can also gather, store, and retrieve information. The basics of information processing go something like this: To be understood, information needs to be received by a receptor and analyzed by an interpreter. Your ears and eyes serve as the main receptors in communication. Your brain is the main interpreter. Without the ears and eyes, the brain would not have sounds and sights to interpret. Without the brain, the neurological impulses sent by the ears and eyes would go unnoticed. The receptors transmit the data. The interpreter figures out what the data mean. The receptors and the interpreter work together so that you can make sense out of your world.

Because the ears, eyes, and brain play such crucial roles in HIP, you need to know a little more about each. Let's look briefly at some of the important aspects of these parts of the physiological system.

THE BRAIN

As the center of interpretation, the brain plays a most important role in HIP. This mass of spongy tissue weighs about three pounds. It is busy attending to the vital bodily functions, such as breathing and heartbeat. It also is the main center for muscle responses and highly complex thought responses. Needless to say, the brain is very important to day-to-day living.

The brain contains 10 to 14 billion nerve cells called *neurons*. Neurons are the smallest unit in the nervous system, and serve as transmitters of electrical-chemical information throughout the brain. Calvin and Ojemann (1980) suggest that neurons are shaped like "leafless trees, with branches and roots separated by a long trunk" (p. 13), and that these neurons act like little computers, relaying messages to one another. Neurons, then, are the basic material of the brain.

Like people, neurons vary in size. Some are as short as one millimeter. Others run from your foot to the base of your brain. No matter what size they are, though, neurons form "families" in that any one neuron can be connected with a number of other neurons. This creates an incredible network of neurons, making it possible for you to think, use language, and interact with others through communication. Without this amazing network of neurons, your intrapersonal communication abilities would be limited severely.

Cerebral Cortex

The brain is made up of many parts, but I will focus on the largest part, the cerebral cortex. As you look at Figure 2.1, you can see that the cortex consists largely of association areas. These are the areas of the brain where ideas and relations form. You think here. You remember stories here. Ideas flash into your mind when these parts of your brain are activated. At the back is the occipital lobe, the area that stores what you see. In the lower center area is the temporal lobe, which is where language processing occurs. Between the visual area (occipital lobe) and the auditory area (temporal lobe) is an association area. This is where what is seen and what is heard can be coordinated.

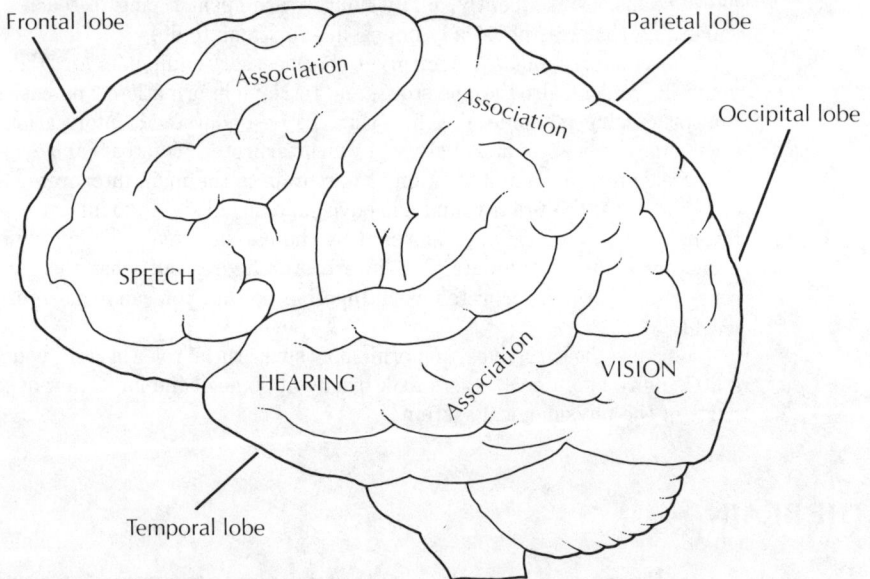

Figure 2.1   The cerebral cortex.

The most important point of this brief description of the cerebral cortex is that your brain is designed for verbal and nonverbal information processing. Put another way, if you didn't have the temporal and occipital lobes to interpret words and gestures, you couldn't communicate as you do. Indeed, damage to these areas of the brain (from an accident or sudden illness) often results in difficulties in speaking and in comprehending speech.

Your brain also affects your memory. Recall that the brain is composed of neurons. These neurons are the main storage units for information, and thus are necessary for memory. However, neurons die, and because they do not replace themselves, the information stored in them is lost. Fortunately, losing *one* neuron may not mean losing the information associated with that neuron because information is most often stored in networks of neurons, rather than in just one. If all the neurons in a network die, however, the information will indeed be lost. Information lost due to neuron decay must be relearned, and relearning implies storing information in other neurons. The effects of dying neurons are seen in people who are senile. Senile people have experienced brain cell losses, making it difficult for them to remember the name of a neighbor or other simple bits of information.

Not only is your brain a living organ that is subject to decay, it is also subject to emotions. Unlike the "brain center" in computers, the human brain has centers of emotion that influence the processing of information. Computers are able to think and reason without emotions; you are not able to do so. Consequently, the information stored in memory is colored by emotions. This means that when you process information, you do so according to your feelings, moods, and attitudes. This provides the "subjective" side of HIP.

Cerebral Lateralization

The picture of the brain in Figure 2.1 is only one side of the story. The brain has two sides, or hemispheres. In essence, each side is a mirror image of the other side. Thus, you have left and right temporal lobes, left and right occipital lobes, etc. The term *cerebral lateralization* simply means that your brain has two hemispheres and that each side is somewhat specialized in its capabilities.

For most people, the left side of the brain controls the language functions (verbal communication). Evidence for the dominance of the left hemisphere for language is found in studies of patients who have suffered brain damage. More than 90 percent of the people with language impairments due to brain damage suffered the damage on the left side of the brain (Geschwind 1970).

The right side of the brain is more adept with visual and spatial tasks and music perception (Moscovitch 1976). This suggests that the right side is better for nonverbal communication, as well (Anderson, Garrison, and Anderson 1979).

It should be pointed out, though, that cerebral lateralization does not mean that the "left side doesn't know what the right side is doing." The two hemispheres are connected by the *corpus callosum*. This is a network of fibers that connects both sides and allows interhemispheric transfer of information. To say that one side is dominant over the other on a specified task is simply to acknowledge that one side of the brain is more adept and complete in handling specific kinds of information. Since we are a highly verbal society that places great emphasis on verbal skills and thinking abilities (as opposed to a heavy emphasis on art), we call the left hemisphere the "major" or more dominant hemisphere. It *is*, but only when you are talking about language functions. On more artistic inputs the right side is dominant.

There is so much more that can be said about the amazing human brain. I have covered the basics so that you might appreciate the work the brain does for you. Without all those neurons with their interconnections, you would certainly be limited in the amount of information that you can store and process. Those 10 to 14 billion neurons go a long way to help you sort the information coming to you every day. Now let's turn to a description of the major receptors for communication, the ears and eyes.

THE EARS AND EYES

Whereas the brain is the main interpreter in HIP, the ears and eyes serve as the main receptors for messages sent by others. Without the ears and eyes sending signals to the brain for processing, it would be impossible to understand what other people are saying to us.

Principles of Sensation

In communication, you rely mostly on hearing (auditory information) and sight (visual information). The other senses of smell, taste, and touch are important but not as central as hearing and sight. Certain principles about the ears and eyes should be kept in mind. First of all, the brain depends on the ears and eyes to send signals for processing. The brain itself doesn't hear or see anything. The receptors do the hearing and seeing, and then they transform the sound waves and light waves into neurochemical impulses to be sent on to the brain for interpretation. Sensation occurs at the receptors (ears and eyes); perception occurs at the brain. Our nervous system serves as the main conduit between the receptors and the brain. This brings me to the second point. Our sensory receptors are specialized. Each is "wired" to receive and translate certain signals. So, the ears hear, and the eyes see. They cannot switch functions. To say that blind people hear better than sighted people is to speak of their heightened *perception* of sounds, not their stronger ears. They are simply more alert to auditory information.

Finally, you should recognize that the quality of the signal sent to the brain for interpretation is a function of the health of the receptor and the strength of the original signal. People who are hard of hearing or who have impaired eyesight recognize the limitations that these defects impose on their ability to receive the signal. Normal hearing and vision assume healthy or corrected receptors. Likewise, the signal itself must have sufficient strength (signal intensity) to activate your ears or eyes. What you learn from this third point is that you really live in a world of sounds and sights that exceed the normal ranges of hearing and vision. There are a lot of things that you don't hear or see. The ear and eye are truly limited receptors in their respective sensory capabilities.

Hearing and Vision

Let's look briefly at the ranges of hearing and vision. Your normal hearing range is about 20 to 20,000 cycles per second (cps). People do not hear as well as some animals. For instance, the household (domestic) cat can hear up to 50,000 cps. The mouse can hear up to 90,000 cps (Nathan 1969). Now you can see why the mouse is such a challenge to the cat! Human vision is even more limited compared with that of other animals. Your visible light spectrum is 400,000 cps (red) to 800,000 cps (violet). But more importantly, your eyes are limited in other ways. You cannot see very well in the dark, but some animals can. You see in a forward direction; you have peripheral vision, but you cannot see behind you. Many birds can. Some birds also have sufficient binocular vision to see a rodent running across a field while they are flying high above the ground. As seeing organisms, humans do not fare well when compared with many animals. If you could hear and see more, you might have a different perspective of your external world. As it stands, you must be satisfied to understand your world within your predetermined limited hearing and vision.

Let's compare the ear and the eye as receptors of information. Coon (1977) estimates that 70 percent of the information conveyed to the brain comes from vision. The amount of information coming from the ears is certainly less than that. This means that your visual capacity is greater than your auditory capacity. The eye's field of input, however, is mostly frontal, whereas the ear's field is omnidirectional (front, side, and back). There may even be differences in how much information the ears and the eyes can take in at one time. When information is presented at a very fast rate (one to two items per second) people remember more items that they hear compared with those that they see. When the rate of presentation is slowed down, people remember about the same amount of information presented to the ears as to the eyes (Laughery and Fell 1969). So at fast rates, your ears outperform your eyes when it comes time to remember what was presented. Most of the time, however, you are not bombarded by information at such fast rates. Combined, the ears and the eyes serve as your "windows to the world," providing much needed information about the world around you.

Coordinated Inputs

As much as the ears and eyes differ from each other, they work together to provide coordinated inputs. This is best illustrated by the phenomenon of reading. Theoretically, reading should be a purely visual experience. Yet most people, when they read, silently say the words to themselves. Reading this way provides both auditory and visual information.

Taking the concept of integration of the ear and the eye farther, you will discover that face-to-face communication consists of analyzing both the speech (auditory) and the actions (visual) of the speaker. When you converse with someone face-to-face you attend to not only what is said (verbal) but how it is said (nonverbal). Hence, the ear and the eye make nicely coordinated receptors for information.

Finally, you should realize that the brain coordinates the information from the ears and eyes. The brain works as a *whole* and combines visual information with auditory information to interpret the message being received. The association areas of the brain make this coordination process possible. Thus, what you hear someone saying and what you see being said can be coordinated and confirmed in the brain (Lennenberg 1967).*

Before you go to the next section ask yourself this question: If you had to choose one, would you prefer to be deaf or blind? Most people would choose deafness over blindness. Apparently, people prefer to see their world more than hear it.

---

*The brain, the ears, and the eyes are far more complex organs than is obvious from our brief discussion. If you are interested in a more detailed discussion, I recommend Peter Nathan's book, *The Nervous System* (1969). He approaches physiology from a communication point of view that makes the physiology easier to digest.

SOME ASSUMPTIONS

Now that you have an understanding of perception and how people are equipped to receive and interpret information, I want to share with you some assumptions that guide my thinking about human information processing. These assumptions originate from the fundamental belief that humans are processors of information. Without the ability to process information, you could not make much sense out of your world. As Bartlett (1932) pointed out years ago, people are, by nature, seekers of meaning. When you seek meaning, you process information. Let's look at three underlying assumptions about HIP.

Active Processing

First, *humans are active processors of information*. The important word here is *active*. This means that you are not like a sponge simply absorbing what is spilled out into the world. Nor are you a container into which life pours experiences. When you encounter information, you can attend to it, ignore it, alter it, or refute it. In other words, when humans process information they actively participate in what happens to that information. You manage and control information as you encounter it.

Unlike animals, you can actually shape your environment. If it gets cold, you can put on a jacket or light the furnace. If someone calls you an abusive name, you can return the "favor" with a choice word of your own. Because you can process information and can communicate in advanced ways, you can act on your world to make it more comfortable for you. In this way, humans are much more advanced than animals. And this is because you and I actively participate in the world of information.

Active participation is especially crucial to communication. For instance, the more you participate in reading this text (taking notes, underlining, disagreeing with me), the more you will learn. The more two people get involved in a conversation, the better the conversation can be. There is no such thing as passive listening and speaking. Communication is an active process.

Structuring Information

The second assumption states that *humans tend to reduce, distort, and structure information*. In the process of trying to make sense out of incoming information, you fit the "new" to the "old." In other words, you relate incoming information to things you have stored in memory. External information is made to fit internal information. This takes place as you assign meaning to incoming messages.

In the process of fitting the incoming information into the existing data stored in memory, you often change the information. This is most graphically illustrated by having someone verbally describe something to you. In order for you to understand it, you must draw a mental picture of the object being described. This is true even if someone shows you photographs of, say, a resort area. It is interesting to observe people's reactions upon visiting such a resort for the first time. They might react like this: "Oh, I didn't expect it to look like this." No matter how much external information (words, photographs) you give people, they will still make your description coincide with what they have in mind. Mental images vary greatly from person to person. As people handle information, they change it, often unknowingly.

Orderliness

The third assumption is that *human beings strive to maintain orderliness in their lives*. I am talking about a cognitive or mental orderliness, not whether you keep your room clean. This assumption suggests that you expect external information to fit neatly into what you already understand. When it doesn't fit well, you work hard to adjust the incoming information so that it coincides with your prior knowledge. Inconsistencies are mentally stressful.

This principle of orderliness is similar to homeostasis in biology. Your body is designed to maintain chemical balance so that you remain healthy. Likewise, "mental" health depends on your ability to reconcile your experiences with your knowledge, feelings, and prior experiences. For instance, if someone announces that tomorrow the sun will rise in the west, you will probably reject such a notion because it contradicts what you already know. To believe such a proposition you would have to alter your prior understanding. Whether you choose to dismiss it as crazy or adopt it as potentially true, you will wrestle with it long enough to settle the matter. Just as your body works for physical harmony, your mind works for psychological harmony. We will discuss this striving for order and harmony more thoroughly in a later chapter. For now, let's simply agree that a large part of information processing is geared toward providing mental order for your life.

SUMMARY

At the very beginning of this book, I said that people have a tendency to take for granted the fundamental intrapersonal processes that allow them to communicate. After reading this chapter, you should have a better appreciation for your own HIP abilities.

The rest of this book will be devoted to exploring in more detail the workings of the intrapersonal processes. As you read each chapter, take time to reflect on how all this applies to you. After all, we are all processors of information.

SUMMARY PROPOSITIONS

1. The brain is your interpreter of information.
2. The brain contains a massive network of neurons that carry information.
3. For most people, the left side of the brain is designed for verbal communication, while the right side works with nonverbal communication.
4. The ears and eyes are the main receptors of information.
5. The receptors send signals to the brain for interpretation.
6. The brain and ears and eyes are uniquely designed to process information for you.
7. Though different, the ear and the eye work together to send messages to the brain indicating *what* is said and *how* it is expressed.

8. There are three assumptions that underlie all human information processing:
   a.   Humans are active processors of information.
   b.   They tend to reduce, distort, and structure information.
   c.   Humans strive to maintain orderliness in their lives.

2 HUMAN INFORMATION PROCESSING

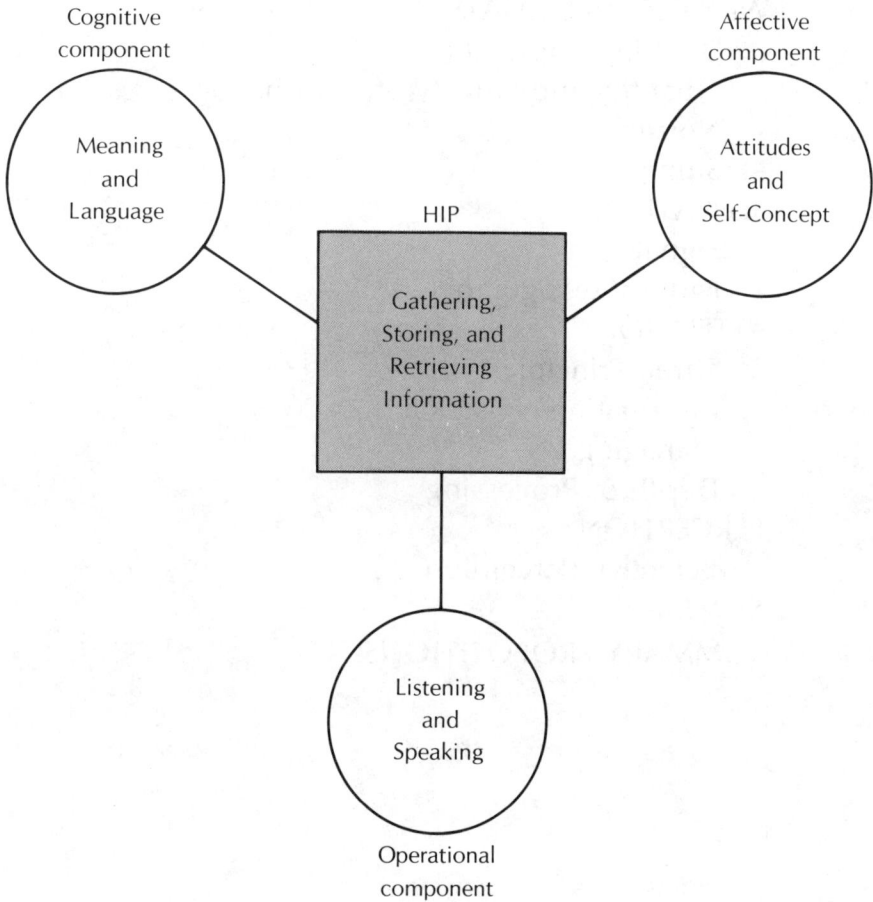

Cognitive
component

Meaning
and
Language

Affective
component

Attitudes
and
Self-Concept

HIP

Gathering,
Storing, and
Retrieving
Information

Listening
and
Speaking

Operational
component

Chapter 3

WHAT IS INFORMATION?
    Defining Information
    Quantity and Quality of Information
    Noise
    Summary
SENSATION
    Signals
    Pattern Recognition
ATTENTION
    Three Principles
    Information/Noise Ratio
    Managing I/N
    Depth of Processing
PERCEPTION
    Selective Perception
SUMMARY
SUMMARY PROPOSITIONS

Gathering Information

Human information processing does not begin until information is gathered. In the last chapter, you learned how you are especially equipped to gather, store, and retrieve information. Now you need a firm understanding of how you gather information. In this chapter, I will define information, and then consider the three fundamental processes underlying information gathering: sensation, attention, and perception. All three work together to make information available to you for processing.

WHAT IS INFORMATION?

There are many ways to think about information. To the electrical engineer, information refers to electrical impulses along a conduit. Most people don't think of information in such a technical sense. Most lay people find information in books, in newspapers, and on the telephone. Whether you think of information in the technical sense or in the more everyday sense, it is clear that information is something that is available to everyone. This implies that information is desirable. In other words, if people seek information, it must be useful to them.

The utility of information comes from its ability to reduce uncertainty in the mind of the receiver. If I tell you that you are reading a book right now, you won't get too excited. There is nothing "new" in my statement to you. It has little information. On the other hand, if I tell you that there is a very attractive person behind you watching your every move, you might get excited. Why? Because it is news. And good news at that. The more a message tells you something that you don't already know, the more information that message has.

Defining Information

Now that you have a general idea about information, I want to offer a more precise definition. Since I am talking about human information processing and not machine information processing, I will present a definition that reflects some of the technical aspects but describes everyday usage of information. _Information is defined as any input that the person attends to for the purposes of reducing uncertainty or confirming prior knowledge_. This definition permits information to serve both learning and confirming roles. When you hear a sound and then turn your head to see what it was, you are seeking information to learn what happened. In this case, you learn something when you discover what caused the sound. On the other hand, you might listen to a phonograph record and follow the lyrics to see whether it is the tune you

23

think it is. By following the lyrics, you can confirm your prior knowledge. In both cases, you are processing information. In the first case, you are doing it for learning. In the second case, you are simply checking up on what you already know.

Quantity and Quality of Information

Information is more than just words or messages. The words or messages have information potential, not information *per se*. People determine the amount of information a message contains. If I tell you that Washington, D. C., is the nation's capital and you already know that, there is little information in such a message. But if I tell you that the University of Oklahoma is located in Norman, Oklahoma, and you didn't know this beforehand, the message is full of information (albeit, not necessarily important information). The point is this: the quantity of information in a message is a product of the receiver's knowledge and need to know.

What kinds of inputs can qualify to be treated as information? One might be tempted to say "only factual data," but this is simply not true. You deal with all kinds of data as though they were information. Humans seem to have few limitations on what they can include as data in daily decision-making. You and I incorporate knowledge, feelings, and expectations as we react and think. As suggested in Chapter 1, both external and internal information qualify to be called information. In sum, there is no such thing as "real" information. You use whatever you can get your intellectual hands on when you process information.

Noise

You can further understand the nature of information by comparing it with noise. Noise is any signal that you do not classify as information. Some stimuli are noise. You actively attend to information. You only monitor noise. As you are reading this book you should be actively attending to the words on this page, yet you are still aware of the fact that other things are going on around you. These other things need only low-level attention from you, and thus they can be monitored rather than carefully processed. How much you attend to something, in many ways, determines just how much information that something has. Unless you classify a signal as noise, it has information. More will be said about information and noise in a later section.

Summary

In summary, then, information is any input that you attend to for the purposes of reducing uncertainty or confirming prior knowledge. Information can be facts, feelings, statistics, or whatever. Data become information when you find it necessary to attend to them. And finally, information is actively processed, whereas noise is simply monitored for continuity.

Now that I have defined information, it is time to turn to gathering information. The major elements of gathering information are sensation, attention, and perception.

SENSATION

People often confuse sensation with perception. When you are sensing, you are hearing, seeing, touching, tasting, and smelling. When you are perceiving, you are interpreting what you have sensed. In human communication, the main senses that you work with are hearing and seeing. The ears and the eyes gather the sensations that are sent to the brain for interpretation. Without sensations, there would be no perceptions of the external world.

Signals

You need to recognize something else about sensations. Since they are physical and not yet psychological, they are not yet meaningful. In other words, sensations are signals, waiting for interpretation. Sensations aren't even noise or information; they are data in waiting. It isn't until you perceive these signals that they begin to take on meaning.

If sensations are waiting to be interpreted, what happens to them? The optic nerve does not send light waves directly to the brain, nor does the auditory nerve send sound waves directly to the brain. These receptors (ears and eyes) *translate* the sound waves and light waves into neural impulses to be sent to the brain. This produces signal alteration. As Norman (1969) pointed out, "the nervous system performs substantial alterations of the physical image received by the sense organs. . . . These transformations . . . simplify tremendously the information that must be transmitted to higher level analyzing systems" (p. 37). By the time the signal is translated by the ears and eyes into nerve impulses to which the brain responds, it is altered so much that it does not at all resemble the original signal. As long as your receptors are healthy and consistent in function, the brain should have little trouble sorting out the signals sent to it. It is important to realize, though, that the brain does not hear or see. It depends on the receptors for input that is relevant to hearing and seeing.

When do sensations begin to take on meaning? That's hard to say, but one of the earliest things that happens to them is that they are recognized for pattern.

Pattern Recognition

Between sensation and attention lies a very crucial cognitive process called pattern recognition. In a nutshell, it is the identification of specific features or attributes of a stimulus that allows proper recognition of a stimulus for what it is. It is your initial, immediate analysis of incoming data. You are using pattern recognition when you discriminate speech sounds from all the other sounds in the world, or when you notice specific body features as you locate your friend in a crowded shopping center.

Since pattern recognition occurs so rapidly, research into this process requires very precise methods of stimulus presentation and response measurement. For the reader interested in this kind of research, Neisser (1967) has several fine chapters on pattern recognition. For our purposes here, let's simply say that pattern recognition is a necessary prerequisite for the upcoming deeper analysis for meaning. Without it, our world would be a blob of undifferentiated noise. With it, we can begin to make sense out of our world.

ATTENTION

You do not attend to all the stimulation that the world presents you; you have to be selective. If you weren't selective, you would go crazy trying to respond to everything around you. Hence, your selective attention processes are crucial to your mental health. Selective attention not only shields you from too many intrusions, it also "puts blinders on your mind," making it difficult to see alternatives.

Three Principles

Because of the role that attention plays in everyday life, you need to recognize immediately three things about attention.

1.   *The number of things to which you can attend at one time is very limited.*   Conscious human attention is finite. Since you have a limited capacity for attention, you must ignore some data, put off others until you are "free" again, or desperately try to expand your momentary capacity. You should not, however, be led into thinking that you can attend to just one thing at a time. Neisser (1976) reminds us that many times we attend to several stimuli at once. It simply depends on the situation.*

2.   *Some things presented to you by the world can go unnoticed or attended to only in an unconscious way.*   As Cherry (1978) noted, you "do not perceive more than a minute fraction of the sights and sounds that fall upon the sense organs: the great majority pass us by" (p. 263). You may often think that you "know" the facts, because you were there. Yet you don't even acknowledge much of the activity going on in your world. This does not, however, mean that you are not affected by that which you don't acknowledge. For instance, you may not be aware of the barometric pressure in the air surrounding you as you read this book, but a sudden change in that pressure could make a big difference, if the change were large enough. You do not have to be aware of stimuli in order to be affected by them.

3.   *The amount of attention given to a stimulus varies according to the difficulty of the task at hand.*   Here is where experience counts. If you are doing something you have done many times before, such as brushing your teeth, then you won't find it necessary to devote a lot of attention to it. On the other hand, if you are giving a speech to a college class on a topic that you have only read about, you will need to spend great amounts of energy to accomplish this task. Public speaking is simply more difficult than brushing your teeth. The more difficult the task, the more energy you are going to have to exert to accomplish it.

Let's summarize the principles about attention. First, human attention is limited in that you cannot handle everything presented to you at once. Second, you won't even notice some stimulation that occurs around you. Third, how much attention you give something depends on how hard the task is for you.

A good way to think of human attention is in terms of information and noise. You classify input as you pay attention to it. Let's see how this process can be described by the information/noise ratio.

Information/Noise Ratio

Active attention involves a certain amount of work. The process of "paying attention" is often misunderstood. Many people believe that paying attention means

---

*Selective attention is also governed by the thalamus. This part of the brain is located below the cerebral cortex, and serves as a gate to control the flow of information into the cerebral cortex.

putting on your perceptual blinders and staring very intently at the stimulus. "Concentrate on what you are doing" is advice given when you are having trouble attending to the message or task at hand. Although this can be good advice, it often misses the mark.

Giving something the attention it needs is not so much a matter of "zeroing in" on the message as it is a matter of successfully screening out interfering stimuli. In other words, before you can pay attention, you must remove distractions. This means that you must make a quick decision about each incoming signal. Since you have a limited amount of energy to spend on incoming messages, you must quickly decide how much each input gets. Some will draw more from you, others less.

How much energy a person chooses to devote to an incoming message is a function of what I call the *information/noise ratio* (I/N). Because you do not have the energy to treat every input as information, you need to make a very fast decision as to the information/noise status of each incoming message. Those things that you judge to be immediately important and relevant will be treated as information. Those things that you can push into the background will be treated as noise. The messages you call information will receive an appropriate amount of energy for active processing. You will attend to these messages and try to understand them. The messages you call noise can simply be monitored. They won't take much energy from your attention "bank."

By determining which input is worth actively attending to, you are able to maintain control over the information that enters your thinking. If you classify too many messages as information, you can experience *information overload*. You have simply given yourself more than you can handle. On the other hand, if you classify most of your inputs as noise because you see them as redundant, uninteresting, or not worth attending to, you will experience *information underload*. You manage your information load by managing your I/N.

The current condition of your I/N is a function of several things. Most important is your "need to know." If you are faced with messages that you need to know about, your I/N will be very selective so that you can attend to the important information and screen out the rest as noise. On the other hand, if you are bored, your I/N will have most of the messages classified as noise.

Managing I/N

One of the more fascinating aspects of the I/N is the relative ease with which you are able to alter it. Shifts in attention can be seen as changes in the values of the numerator and denominator of the I/N. This is best illustrated by Colin Cherry's "cocktail party problem." Cherry (1953) points out that people seem to be able to attend selectively to a number of messages at one time, while actively participating in only one of them. When you are in a crowded room with a lot of conversations going on simultaneously, you are able to monitor several conversations while "carrying your weight" in only one of them.

How are you able to follow a number of conversations at once? As you shift your attention from one conversation to another do you ignore the other conversations? What happens to the unattended messages? Do you hear them? The answer is "Yes." But you listen quite selectively to the other conversations. You simply monitor them for noticeable changes. You listen for changes in sound caused by major topic shifts, major changes in the emotional intensity of the conversation, or perhaps a noticeable addition or deletion of people from the circle of talk.

Selective attention often occurs without our realizing it. I remember once sitting down to read a novel while my daughter was watching TV in the same room less than ten feet from me. At first I would read a line or two, then look up at the TV, and then go back to the book, only to return to the TV within a few seconds. After bobbing like this for awhile, I finally settled down to read and ignored the TV. How did this occur? Did I unconsciously scold myself with the admonishment that it is better to read literature than it is to be captivated by the tube? That's possible, but I think I finally altered my I/N, making the TV input noise so that the novel became information. Until I was able to do so, I was unable to devote enough energy to the novel. It is important to note that it is the *rejection* of unwanted input (cognitively classifying it as noise), not the serious "homing in" on the wanted message, that made it possible for me to read the novel.

But what about the TV? Did I go deaf to it? No. In fact, I did look up later as my attention was abruptly drawn away from the book. And do you know why? You got it—a commercial.

Why did the commercial cause me to look up? Do I have some affinity for commercials? Absolutely not! As I was reading the novel, I was also monitoring the TV program for repeated patterns of input (dialogue, background music). As long as the same patterns emerged, I did not carefully attend to the TV. But as soon as the dialogue or music made a major shift, I shifted my attention. I am sure that this same thing has happened to you.

Depth of Processing

Responding to something that you have classified as noise takes less energy than responding to something classified as information. The reason for this is centered in *depth of processing*, or how thoroughly you analyze a message. Some messages need only to be monitored; others need more time and careful study. For instance, as I type this manuscript I need to choose my words carefully. This means that I must process my ideas more deeply as I am typing them on this page. On the other hand, the rumble from my air conditioner, the humming sound of my electric typewriter, and the children playing outside must be classified as noise and not processed very deeply. Similarly, I must not be distracted by the radio playing in the next room. If I attend to the radio, I take away from my limited attention that I need for preparing this text.

Craik and Lockhart (1972) tell us that people can achieve three levels as they process information. The first level requires recognizing the signal itself. At this level you simply recognize the message and acknowledge its presence. Level two occurs when you assign meaning to the incoming message. In other words, you analyze the content of the message to discover the idea being presented. The third level goes beyond assigning meaning. This occurs when you take the message content and relate it to other things stored in your memory. It is at the third level that you form verbal associations. For instance, the message may remind you to do something else later, or you might look for similarities in the content of the message with things you already know. The third level is, in essence, a reflective level. You reflect not only on the content of the message, but on its implications as well.

What all this implies is that at any given time the number of items you have in the numerator in the I/N ratio will probably be smaller than the number of items you have in the denominator. Since you can reach level three in processing information and since this takes more time and energy, it makes sense to keep the numerator smaller than the denominator. Furthermore, since noise takes less energy to monitor than does information, you can have many items of noise in the denominator while having fewer items of information in the numerator. In a nutshell, altering the I/N ratio is an efficient way to handle many messages at once.

PERCEPTION

Since I discussed perception in Chapter 1, you are already familiar with some of its workings. As defined there, perception is organizing your sensations into recognizable wholes. By organizing I mean grouping. You are bombarded by sensations all the time. Somehow you must know when one begins and another ends, or you must decide which sensation goes with what other sensation to produce a thing that you recognize. Perceptions are clusters of grouped sensations that combine to make the resulting product recognizable. Applied to communication, you have verbal and nonverbal sensations of sounds and movements that must somehow be combined to be seen as spoken words, sentences, and speeches so that they become meaningful. When you apply meaning to your sensations, you are perceiving; you are giving psychological order to your sensations. In doing so, you rely on at least two things—your meanings and your feelings. As you perceive something, you decide not only what it means, but how you feel about it as well. As you saw earlier, your meanings and feelings create expectations. Thus, you see what you expect to see. Perceptions are a combination of your sensations plus your meanings plus your feelings. Figure 3.1 illustrates this point.

Figure 3.1   The parts of perception.

When you apply perception to human communication, you become keenly aware of the contributions of each of the surrounding components (cognitive, affective, and operational) to basic HIP. For instance, you get your meanings from the cognitive component. Your feelings come from the affective component. And finally, you perceive through the listening part of the operational component. All three components contribute to communication and to your perceptions.

Selective Perception

Just as you can have selective attention, you have selective perception. You selectively perceive what you are prepared to perceive. Your expectations determine "what should be there." If you are looking for something that you have misplaced, it will take very little data to signal its presence to you when you first locate it. Your perceptual mind-set will help you spot the lost item immediately. If you are trying to locate your car in a parking lot, you don't need to see the whole car before you recognize it.

Your perceptual mind-set can be stimulated and built by someone else. As you communicate with others, they affect how you see the world. I remember once a friend telling me how the quality of lumber had dropped in recent years. I hadn't noticed, but I stored that bit of information away and resurrected it in the lumberyard four months later. He was right; the lumber was worse than I remembered from years before. What my friend did was give me a perception that I was able to use later. That is one of the by-products of communication. The more you communicate with other people, the more you exchange perceptions about the world around you.

SUMMARY

Information gathering includes sensation, attention, and perception. Although I have talked about them separately, they work conjointly and very rapidly. In fact, it is almost impossible to separate attention from perception. You perceive what you attend to, but you also attend to what you perceive. Sensations are the raw data of HIP. They are the sights and sounds that the eyes and ears detect. The brain depends on these receptors to provide sensations for interpretation.

Attention is selective by nature, and successful attention means discarding unwanted input so that you can focus on the wanted information. How you vary your attention was described by the I/N ratio. The more attention a message needs, the more the other items of input have to be downplayed to noise. Finally, perception is a product of your sensations, meanings, and feelings.

SUMMARY PROPOSITIONS

1. Information is any input that a person attends to for the purposes of reducing uncertainty or confirming prior knowledge.
2. Information is more than words.
3. We incorporate both internal and external sources of information.
4. Data become information when you decide that they are worth attending to.
5. Information is actively processed, whereas noise is simply monitored.
6. We process any data twice—first in a general way, then in a more analytic way.
7. We are affected by external inputs whether we are aware of them or not.
8. Sensations are the raw data provided by our sensory receptors.
9. In communication, the main sensations come from the ears and eyes.
10. Sensations are altered before the brain processes them.
11. Attention is the process of filtering out the unwanted signals so that you can process the wanted ones.
12. The number of things that we attend to at one time is very limited.
13. Some things presented to us by the world go unnoticed or are attended to only in an unconscious way.
14. The amount of attention given to a stimulus varies according to the difficulty of the task.
15. Paying attention is altering the information/noise ratio (I/N).
16. It takes more energy to attend to information than it does to monitor noise.
17. Perception = sensations + meanings + feelings.

Chapter 4

SHORT-TERM MEMORY
   Duration
   Rehearsal
   Chunking
   Forgetting
LONG-TERM MEMORY
   Accessibility
   Organization
   Forgetting
STM AND LTM COMPARED
SUCCESSFUL STORAGE
RECALLING INFORMATION
KINDS OF REMEMBERING
   Recognition
   Cued Recall
   Noncued Recall
MESSAGE DISTORTIONS
   Primacy-Recency
   Leveling, Sharpening, and Assimilation
SUMMARY
SUMMARY PROPOSITIONS

Storing and Retrieving Information

Gathering information is only the beginning to HIP. Now information must be stored and made ready for retrieval. If it is not stored, it cannot be used later. In this chapter, I will discuss short-term memory and long-term memory and then compare the two. After considering what helps you successfully store information, I will examine recalling information. Following that will be a discussion of the kinds of remembering and how messages get distorted.

If information that is gathered is not stored, it will get lost. How people store information is a most intriguing area of research. Since storing information takes place inside your head, it is difficult to observe this process firsthand. Consequently, research has left us with more questions than answers about human information storage. Researchers do know, however, that there are two memory systems — short-term memory (STM) and long-term memory (LTM).

SHORT-TERM MEMORY

Short-term memory refers to a temporary "holding station" for information before you use it or send it on to long-term memory. You use STM everyday. When you take notes in class, you use STM. As the instructor talks, you mentally rehearse and write down what is said. In a conversation, you use STM to keep track of what is being said as you exchange ideas with someone else.

Duration

Most people agree that STM lasts anywhere from 10 to 30 seconds. In reality, the duration of STM depends on the task at hand. Since STM is a "working" memory or holding station, it can last as long as you make it last. For very well-learned tasks at which you have lots of prior experience, you don't need a very long STM. But for new tasks that you have never encountered before, you will need a longer STM.

Rehearsal

How do you make STM last? It is a matter of rehearsal. The primary function of STM is to hold information in "suspension" long enough so that you can use it or store it in LTM. Trying to remember a phone number you found in the directory while you dig for the necessary change in your pocket or purse is an instance of STM at work. As you search for your money, you need to repeat the number to yourself (silently or aloud) so you don't forget it. Sometimes you may rehearse a number, then dial it, only to discover that you reached the wrong number. Remember this: You will recall whatever you rehearse. So be sure that you have your information correct before you rehearse it. If you do not rehearse, you will not remember. Probably more than any other concept, rehearsal is the key to recall in STM.

Chunking

Given that rehearsal is central to recall in STM, do you have to rehearse everything you encounter word-for-word? The answer to this question is a qualified "No." I say "qualified" because a certain amount of sound rehearsal takes place in STM. But your task is typically not to remember the exact words, but to try to remember ideas. If you had to remember each signal exactly as it was presented, you would be too busy to get much understanding done. With STM you usually look for clusters of input that are easier to remember than the individual units. Let's get back into the phone booth for a minute. There are seven digits in a phone number (if you don't need the area code). You can rehearse these digits as seven separate numbers, or you can group them into one set of three numbers, followed by another set of four numbers. Rehearsing the numbers as sets is a form of *chunking*.

Chunking refers to the grouping of a number of smaller units into one larger unit in order to aid recall. This was demonstrated by Miller (1956), who found that most people could recall 7 ± 2 units of information out of STM. Those who were able to group the inputs into chunks recalled 7 ± 2 chunks, and each chunk contained more than one single item of information. Consequently, chunking led to more total recall.

Forgetting

In spite of rehearsal and successful chunking of input, forgetting still occurs in STM. Why? The answer to this question is twofold: You forget because of *item decay* (information gets lost over time) and *interference*. Item decay occurs when you fail to use information that you have learned, or when the information you learned was not well rehearsed to begin with. In essence, you simply forget information that is not properly stored; it decays.

More intriguing than the decay process is the interference process. Interference occurs when the recall of one item is made more difficult because of the distraction of other things you are trying to remember as well. Interference can occur at the time of input if you are bombarded with too many things to remember at one time (information overload). Interference also occurs if an item of input is very similar to another item not present at the time of input. Studies by Waugh and Norman (1965), Wickelgren (1965), and Wicken and Clark (1968) show that forgetting in STM is a function not only of decay but also of interference. People can get confused if there is too much similarity between items that are remembered separately. For instance, it is often easier to recall unlike items like your phone number and the name of your pet dog than it is to recall the names of two different songs that sound alike. These researchers confirmed that when items sounded alike or meant similar things it was harder for the subjects to keep them straight.

In summary, then, STM is highly dependent on rehearsal, chunking, usage, and a relative lack of interference. If you rehearse, look for a way to organize the information, use the information immediately, and avoid confusions, you should be able to recall accurately informati presented to your STM.

LONG-TERM MEMORY

LTM is your main memory bank, your permanent memory. Here is where you have stored your childhood memories, the Pledge of Allegiance, facts needed to pass an exam, knowledge, meanings. Modern neurologists believe that the brain is capable of storing *all* the information you have ever received. This creates a permanent record of all the experiences you have ever had. But this doesn't mean that you can remember it all.

Having information stored and being able to recall it are two different matters. Recently I met a former student coming out of the library. We talked for five or six minutes, and throughout that time I couldn't remember his name. I know that I knew it, because I make a point of addressing my students by their names. What happened? There are a number of possibilities, but one reason that seems evident is interference. I have learned many other students' names since he and I were in class together, and these later names crowded my immediate recall of his name. If I could have had a unique tag to associate with him, I might have remembered his name. Unless you find a way to isolate an item in memory, it can simply blend into the array of other memories. The more unique an item is, the easier it will be to recall later—or, the more accessible it will be.

Accessibility

Failure to recall information out of LTM is seen as a problem of *accessibility*, or the ease with which you remember an item. The information in LTM is vast, and it is waiting to be recalled. If you fail to recall something that happened to you long ago, it is because you are not using the correct *cue* for recall. Unless you have the right prompting (reminders), or unless you have information that is unique, you will have difficulty recalling most of what you have stored in LTM. If in my conversation with the student at the library he had given me something to "jog" my memory, I might have remembered his name. Unfortunately, it didn't happen.

The problem of accessibility is also dependent on what Tulving and Osler (1968) call *encoding specificity*. This term simply means that whenever you learn something new, you store it (encode it) along with another idea you already have in LTM. For instance, your memories of learning to swim may be stored with your image of a river where you first were taught to swim. These two ideas (learning to swim and the river) are encoded (stored) together in memory. Whenever you are reminded of swimming, you should think about the river as well. What all this implies is that if someone gives you a cue of "swimming," that should call up the specific association of the river. As Tulving and Osler suggest, you cannot get an idea out of a person's memory until you hit the specific association that is encoded along with that idea. Many TV game shows are based on ideas associated in memory. *Password* is such a game.

The idea that you can recall anything that happened to you years ago brings us to an interesting problem of defining forgetting and memory. Researchers test memory through recall. If people in such studies do not recall something, researchers assume that it is forgotten. Whether the item is truly lost is unknown. This means that forgetting is more a matter of unsuccessful recall than it is a loss of previously stored information. If you can't remember something, it is not necessarily gone from your memory. You just can't get to it. Except in instances of senility, it is difficult to know for sure when someone has truly lost or forgotten something that was once stored in LTM.

Organization

In many ways, your ability to recall something from LTM depends not only on its accessibility but on its organization as well. In STM, you saw that chunking was the primary method of organization. In LTM, you have at least two kinds of organization. Endel Tulving (1972) identifies these as episodic and semantic organization.

Episodic organization assumes that you store things as complete events (like your phone number). Hence, you can accurately recite the Lord's Prayer or tell a story that describes what you did last night. According to Tulving, organizing your memories into episodes helps keep things in order. The underlying order in episodic organization is probably according to chronology or appearance. Your memory for tying your shoes is stored in an episodic pattern. Your image of your hometown is stored episodically.

Not all memories are stored according to time order or appearance. Some ideas must be stored by meaning. Tulving calls this *semantic* organization. Our conceptual memory is organized semantically. Words that are similar in meaning are stored in close association with one another. Words that are frequently used together are stored together in semantic LTM. Semantic LTM is a major category system. Your understanding of concepts, ideas, and meanings is stored semantically.

Semantic organization makes it possible for you to form ideas and talk about them and to decipher someone else's message. The precise organization of semantic LTM is still under investigation. But we do know that ideas are not just randomly scattered throughout your brain. Some order exists, even if by simple associations.

By having both kinds of organization in LTM, you have dual capabilities. You can recall events (piece together a story), and you can recall ideas (tell what you know about something). This dual capability gives you quite a bit of flexibility in processing information. Without episodic organization, you would have difficulty telling stories. Without semantic organization, you would have difficulty understanding messages.

Forgetting

How does forgetting occur in LTM? There are two strains of research that attempt to answer this question. One way of forgetting is called *retroactive interference*, while the other is *proactive interference*.

Studies of retroactive interference have subjects learn a list of, say, ten words. When all have memorized the list, half of them are given a new list of words to learn. After they have learned the second list, they are given a recall test of the first list. The other half is excluded from having to learn the second list, but is given the test on the first list at the same time as the others. The two groups' recall scores of list one are compared. If the group that had to learn the additional list of words remembers fewer words from the first list than does the other group that didn't have to cope with list two, then we say that learning the second list interfered with remembering the first list. This is exactly what Jenkins and Dallenbach (1924) found. Studies like this one show that new learning has the potential to interfere with earlier learning. This retroactive interference occurs most often when the new task is similar to the prior task but not identical in content.

On the other side of the research coin is the work on proactive interference. Here the hypothesis is that prior learning (if well learned) will interfere with the learning of new material, especially if there is a lot of similarity between the two tasks. Underwood (1957) found that the more people had to remember from earlier lists of words, the harder it was for them to recall the most immediate list they learned. This points to the familiar problem of overload. If you are asked to remember more than one list of words, you are likely to have lower recall scores for the later lists. It's like going to the grocery store without a list of items written down. Your chances of forgetting some of the items are greatly increased as the list lengthens.

Given that research has shown both retroactive and proactive interference effects in LTM, you might be asking which one is correct? On the surface they appear to be contradictory findings. In reality, though, they point to the same problem, that is, the inability to successfully discriminate two or more items for memory. Whether new learning interferes with remembering past learning or vice versa, the problem is the same. How do you keep things separated so that they retain their respective uniqueness? As you will discover in the upcoming chapter on meaning, you make early decisions about the distinctive features of items so that you know not only what something *is* but what it *is not*. How good you are at this task determines how much information you can handle at one time. In order to inhibit the effects of both kinds of interference, you should always look for the unique characteristics of objects as well as pay attention to the fundamental defining characteristics of the objects. People who sell and promote commercial techniques for increasing memory skills center their teaching on how to make inputs more unique so that they are easier to recall.

STM AND LTM COMPARED

As you can tell by now, there are some similarities in successful recall whether the information comes from STM or LTM. There are, however, some notable differences between the two systems of memory. The chart below provides a convenient comparison of STM and LTM.

	STM	*LTM*
Purpose:	Temporary storage	Permanent storage
Working Rate:	Fast	Slow
Size:	7±2 items	Unlimited
Duration:	Very brief	Unlimited
Organization:	Chunking	Episodic and semantic

As the chart shows, STM and LTM differ in terms of purpose, working rate, size, duration, and organization. Rather than review each comparison separately, let me remind you that STM is a very fast-working memory that holds information so that it can be either stored in LTM or used. LTM is a permanent memory that catalogues your inputs according to its existing category system. LTM is slower than STM, because finding the right storage point for incoming information takes time. Whereas STM quickly fades without rehearsal, LTM seems to endure great lengths of time.

SUCCESSFUL STORAGE

From a practical standpoint, you might be wondering what you can do to improve your ability to store information, whether in STM or LTM. Some things that lead to successful storage of information have been mentioned already, but it would be a good idea to highlight four items. Successful storage of information is dependent on:

1. *Rehearsal:* New information must be rehearsed long enough to figure out where it belongs in LTM. Failing to rehearse can lead to loss of data.

2. *Meaningfulness:* New information needs to be made meaningful so that it may be stored in memory. The more readily you assign meaning to the input, the more likely it will be stored.

3. *Codability:* Input must be recognizable. You need a ready code to translate input into meaningful units. For instance, the numbers 18121776 can be coded into two sets of numbers that read 1812 and 1776.

4. *Multichannel Inputs:* Data that are both seen and heard have a greater chance of being stored than data that come to the brain from only one sensory input. This is called the *dual-coding hypothesis*.

These four notions are not the only things that influence information storage. But if you consciously apply each one as you are learning new information, you should increase the likelihood of successfully storing your new information. For those who are interested in other recommendations applying to note-taking and studying for exams, see the Appendix of this book.

RECALLING INFORMATION

Now that you have successfully stored information, how do you get it out? It isn't simply a matter of searching out all you know about a subject and then parroting what you have stored. Information retrieval is characterized by selection and reconstruction. *Selection* means that you pick and choose details from your memory. *Reconstruction* means that you take the information you have chosen and piece together a "story" or idea that makes sense. In all cases, recall (retrieved information) is incomplete. You rarely recall information completely intact as you learned it.

Why are people generally selective and reconstructive? Why can't you "tell it like it is?" Sometimes you can, but most of the time you can't. Human recall is limited by many factors that make it difficult for you to recall information exactly as you have it stored. For instance, you may fail to remember one part of something because it wasn't learned well enough in the first place. Another reason might be your attitudes about the subject. You might dislike childbeaters so much that it is hard for you to remember any good qualities about such a person.

As you will continue to discover throughout this book, your ability to recall information is a function of the cognitive, affective, and operational components that surround your basic HIP ability. Each one of these intrapersonal components influences how you selectively reconstruct your recall. Much more will be said about recall in the chapter on speaking. For now, let's look at three kinds of remembering.

KINDS OF REMEMBERING

One of the things that affects how complete recall will be is how recall is generated. By this I mean that you can produce recall under a number of different circumstances. For instance, you may think of something because someone else reminded you of it. That is a form of cued recall. Other times, you get ideas without any particular prompting from someone. This is called free recall. Let's look at the kinds of remembering to see how they affect the completeness of memory retrieval.

Recognition

This is the kind of remembering wherein you are given a choice of answers and asked to identify the correct one. Multiple-choice exams can be an example of recognition-type remembering. Another example would be recognizing your coat in a closet full of coats. When you walk into your classroom, you should recognize the room, the other people, and the instructor. Thus, recognition memory is matching what you see with what you know.

Cued Recall

This kind of remembering is dependent on cues from you or someone else. Cued recall occurs when you have been reminded of an item of information. You are using cued recall when someone says something such as, "Do you remember the name of the restaurant where we had sourdough french bread with our meal?" The questioner is giving you hints to help remind you of the name of the restaurant. Mentioning the bread is a way of cuing you. How successful the cue is depends on whether you stored the cue in your mind with the name of the restaurant (encoding specificity). The difference between recognition and cued recall is in the information provided in the inquiry. Recognition-type remembering has the answer in the question. Cued recall uses hints. But you still must dig out your answer from memory.

Noncued Recall

In noncued recall there are no hints and the correct answer is not among a group of given answers. In noncued recall you do all the work. A good example of noncued recall is an essay exam. When you answer an essay question, not only must you provide the information requested, you must organize it as well. The same is true of any noncued recall situation: You provide the information and you organize it.

Of these three kinds of remembering, recognition is the easiest. Noncued recall is the most difficult. You can remember more things by recognizing them than you can by recalling them straight from your memory. This means that recognition memory is a better measure of how much you know, while noncued recall is a better measure of how you have your information organized and what you feel is important.

In terms of human communication, cued recall is the most evident kind of remembering. As people interact with one another, they cue each other's memories. I say something, and that reminds you of something to say when it is your turn to talk. By talking with other people, you activate your memory and the memories of your companions. And that is one of the key functions of human communication. So in terms of human communication, cued recall is the kind of remembering that applies the most.

MESSAGE DISTORTIONS

If recall is selective and reconstructive, and if you use cued recall methods for expressing yourself during communication, what does the output look like? Do you produce messages that are incomplete and distorted? The answer is "Yes." In a later chapter, I will deal more thoroughly with speech output, but for now let me point out two general ways you produce incomplete and distorted messages.

Primacy-Recency

First of all, you must understand that information retrieval is not a very "level" process. In other words, as you are recalling something there will be times in your story that your recall is nearly perfect. There will be other points in your story that are sketchy at best. As you look back on your completed recall, you will discover that you left things out and that certain points were more developed than others. It is almost impossible to maintain a steady, high rate of recall throughout a whole story. In fact, research shows that details at the beginning and at the end of a story will be easier to remember than those details in the middle (Rosnow 1966). This is called the *primacy-recency* effect. Because people have trouble remembering all parts of a story, event, or idea with equal accuracy, they produce incomplete messages.

Leveling, Sharpening, and Assimilation

Whenever people recall information, they distort it. This was especially evident in Allport and Postman's (1945) work on rumors. They found that as people passed on information to each other, they changed it. Such is the nature of rumors. But even our daily interactions have distortions in them. Therefore, you need to be aware of how information can be distorted in everyday communication.

Allport and Postman identified three kinds of information distortion:

1. *Leveling:*   This occurs when some of the original information is missing, thereby making the message shorter and simpler.
2. *Sharpening:*   This occurs when some of the minor points become major points and are made to be more important than they were originally.
3. *Assimilation:*   This occurs when the story is rearranged to make more sense. Interpretations are added, along with some inferences. All of this is done to help the story fit some kind of theme.

As these findings tell us, when you recall information you are likely to make it simpler (leveling), organized around a few points (sharpening), and sensible (assimilation). In other words, your recall can be seen as a story.

Whenever you tell a story, you have a whole idea or event in mind. As you are relating your information to someone else, you talk as though you are thinking in paragraphs rather than words. You know where you are going; you just hope that you don't forget anything along the way. Unfortunately, as you lean on your memory and on your ability to speak to reconstruct what you have in mind, you distort information. Most of the time you don't realize that you are twisting the facts a bit. It just happens. Human recall is rarely free from bias.

SUMMARY

The ability to store and retrieve information is critical for human information processing. How you have information stored determines, in part, how you retrieve it. When storing information you take advantage of two memory systems—STM and LTM. Both work together, but have different functions for memory in general. STM is primarily a temporary way station until you decide to use the information or send it on to LTM. In order to inhibit forgetting in STM you must rehearse information. Rehearsing information also increases the chances of successfully storing it in LTM. Rehearsal, then, helps both STM and LTM. In order to make memory more efficient, it is a good idea to chunk the information. You should also look for things that make any input unique. The more unique the input, the more likely you will be able to recall it later. The permanent memory, LTM, is like a huge catalogue of events (episodic organization) and concepts (semantic organization). Episodes are organized by time and space. Concepts are organized by meaningful associations. Ideas that go together in thoughts go together in LTM as well. Any new item will be stored in LTM if it fits prior experience. As with STM, interference is one of the major causes of forgetting.

Retrieving information is not a matter of dumping your memory into messages. Rather, recall is selective and reconstructive. You selectively piece together things you remember to form a sensible message. How you retrieve something is often a function of the kind of remembering you are doing at the moment. In human communication, cued recall is one of the main methods for memory. People cue each other as they talk. Finally, no matter how you are being cued (if at all) you will produce messages that are distorted and that fall short of everything you know about the topic. It is nearly impossible to say everything you know about any subject at any one time.

SUMMARY PROPOSITIONS

1. We have two memories—STM and LTM.
2. STM is a temporary memory designed to hold information in suspension.
3. LTM is a permanent memory that is used for storing information for later use.
4. STM and LTM depend on rehearsal.
5. Interference causes us to forget items in both STM and LTM.
6. STM works best when information is grouped into chunks.
7. LTM works best when information can easily be stored in one of the pre-existing categories.
8. LTM has two organizations—episodic and semantic.
9. Both retroactive and proactive interference can cause forgetting in LTM.
10. The more unique the information is, the easier it will be to recall later.
11. Successful storage of information is enhanced by:
    a. rehearsal
    b. meaningfulness

        c.   codability

        d.   multichannel inputs

12. Retrieving information is selective and reconstructive.

13. Of the three kinds of remembering, cued recall best describes the kind found in human communication.

14. We distort information when we retrieve it.

15. Allport and Postman found three kinds of distortion—leveling, sharpening, and assimilation.

3 COGNITIVE COMPONENT

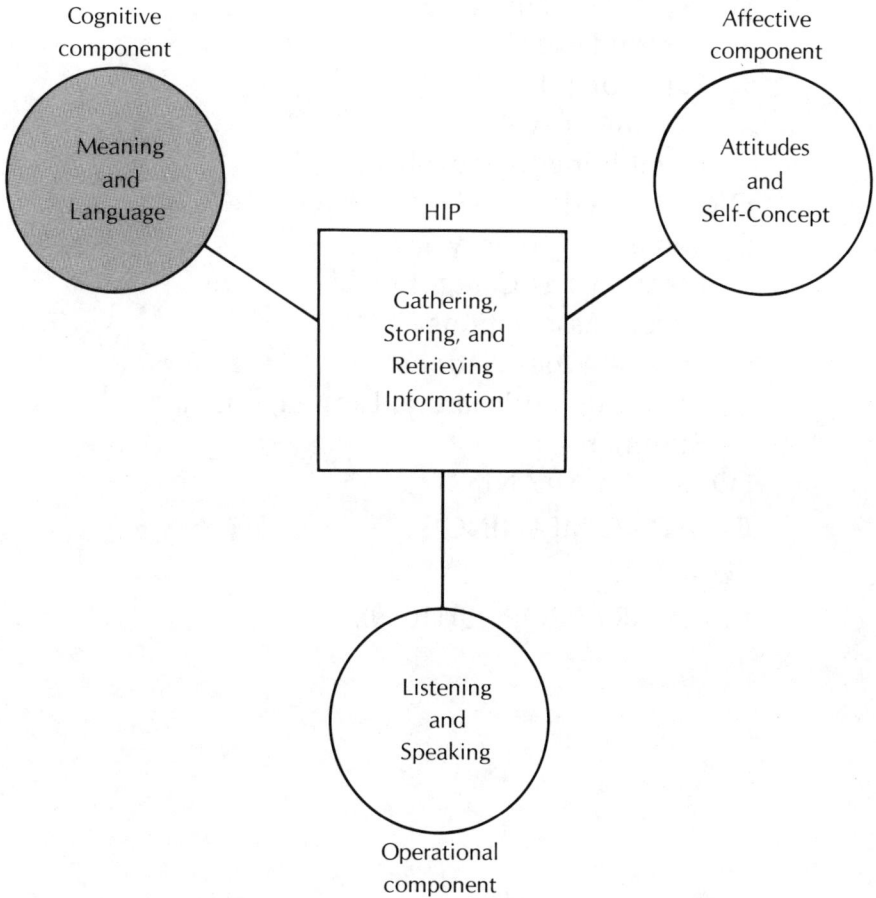

Cognitive
component

Meaning
and
Language

Affective
component

Attitudes
and
Self-Concept

HIP

Gathering,
Storing, and
Retrieving
Information

Listening
and
Speaking

Operational
component

Chapter 5

WHAT IS MEANING?
    Formal Level
    Functional Level
    Affective Level
    Combining the Levels
ORGANIZATION OF MEANING
    Semantic Memory
    Meanings as Categories
    Verbal Associations
    Learning Associations
    Meanings and Natural Language Usage
    Summary
FORMS OF MEANING
CREATING MEANING
SUMMARY
SUMMARY PROPOSITIONS

Meaning

When it comes to processing information, the difference between humans and computers is significant, especially concerning the topic of *meaning*. Computers analyze data without reference to meaning. Humans, on the other hand, are very conscious of meaning as they process information. We are, after all, seekers of meaning.

Because meaning is so important in *human* information processing, you need to know more about this part of the cognitive component. After defining meaning, I will describe how you have meanings organized in your memory. Then I will deal with three forms of meaning. Finally, I will look at how people must create meaning as they interact with one another.

In the model presented in Chapter 1, I suggested that three major areas (cognitive, affective, and operational) surround the central system of gathering, storing, and retrieving information. Within the cognitive elements that influence HIP are meaning and language. Some argue that meaning is what HIP is "about" and that language is the basic mechanism for expressing meaning.

To call meaning and language "cognitive" indicates that they are elements of the mind. In other words, meanings are not dictionary entries, nor is language conceived of as the diagram of a sentence. When speaking of meaning I will be talking about concepts you understand in your head. When I deal with language I will be concerned with your knowledge of the rules of language as evidenced by your ability to speak and write, as well as listen and read. To say that someone speaks meaningfully implies that meaning underlies his or her speech. To say that someone speaks correctly implies that the person is knowledgeable of the rules of language. This chapter will examine meaning to see how it fits into your ability to process information and communicate effectively.

WHAT IS MEANING?

Without question, the meaning of meaning is tricky business. Let's take a look at how meaning is conceived from the HIP perspective. First of all, you must recognize that meanings are based on perceptions. They are internal information. They are part of the products of perception. Meanings are not definitions in the formal sense. When you interact with others, you do not communicate definitions. You use words to signal concepts that you have in mind. Because meanings are based on perceptions and because perceptions are personal, meanings are personal. They remain within you when you use words to form messages. More specifically, meanings are seen as representing your understanding of the formal, functional, and affective levels of the topic in question.

45

Formal Level

When you understand things at the *formal* level, you know what they are and what attributes they have. This is sometimes called *denotative* meaning. Formal, denotative meaning is necessary for simple identification processes. Imagine what it would be like if you didn't have enough formal meaning to find your car in a parking lot or to locate your coat in a cloakroom at a restaurant.

Frank Smith, a Canadian psychologist, describes the formal level of meaning as having two parts—class inclusion and property relations (Smith 1975). *Class inclusion* refers to your ability to identify an object as a member of a category of things you already know so that when you see something you can say, "That is a _____." For instance, you might say, "Louise is a woman." Here you are expressing your understanding that Louise is a female, as opposed to being a male. This is called your *ISA* aspect of meaning, because you know that each person, place, or thing "isa" something. The second part of Smith's system, the *property relations*, designates the attributes of things. If you say, "My car has a clutch," this denotes your understanding of one of the defining features of your car. It is through property relations that you are able to tag things you know to make them distinguishable from each other. As Smith points out, the meaning of any concept must take note of that concept's defining characteristics. So in order to identify your friend Louise, you will need to know that she is a woman and that she has certain attributes that identify her from others. You need to know what Louise has, or *HASA*. If you understand what something is (ISA) and what it must have (HASA), then you are on your way to having formal meaning for the topic at hand.

Functional Level

The ISA and HASA aspects of meaning are sufficient for examining the formal level, but the *functional* level requires additional information about the topic. To say that you have a functional understanding about something is to say that you know what something does or what it is used for. In other words, you not only know its state (formal) but you know its usage (functional) as well. To describe how a turntable on a stereo looks is sufficient for finding it in a room cluttered with other objects, but to say that you play records on it is quite another matter. Then you are talking about how to use the turntable. By understanding that the turntable plays records you know what it does. Thus, you know what it *DOESA*.

Affective Level

Thus far, your understanding of meaning combines the formal and the functional. You know what "X" ISA, HASA, and DOESA. One final level of understanding is necessary to complete your understanding of meaning. It is called the *affective* level.

Often called *connotative* meaning, the affective level of meaning refers to your attitudes about things. For example, when you think about your stereo component system, you not only know what it looks like and what it does, you have feelings about it as well. Your feelings about your stereo are just as important as your formal and functional meanings about the equipment. For instance, if you paid over $500 for your stereo equipment and if that is a lot of money to you, you are likely to see your system as "expensive" and "worthy of careful treatment." Now if your roommate is unimpressed by your investment, and is known for setting a drippy glass on your speakers, the two of you are likely to have different affective feelings for your stereo system.

You both may have similar formal and functional understandings about your equipment, but widely divergent opinions about it. (If that's the case, keep that clown away from your stereo!)

Combining the Levels

Returning to the original question ("What is meaning?"), you can now say that it is made up of three levels of understanding (formal, functional, and affective). And all three combine to make up meanings for things you encounter everyday. As a way of remembering the three levels of meaning, you might ask yourself the following questions while trying to figure out what something means:

Level A, Formal: What is this? What are its attributes?
Level B, Functional: What does it do?
Level C, Affective: How do I feel about it?

One final point before leaving the definition of meaning: To say that you know what something is, what it has, what it does, and how you feel about it, implies that you also know what it is not, has not, and does not. In other words, when you make decisions about the meaning of something, you establish both the positive and negative sides of meaning. For instance, if an object is hard, it can't be soft. If it is inanimate, it can't be alive. If it is good, then it cannot be bad. Clear meanings demand clear discriminations.

ORGANIZATION OF MEANING

If meanings represent, in part, a record of your past experiences and if they must be learned, how are they stored in memory? Is your brain like a tape recorder, taking in signals and recording them in the order received? When that "tape" is played back, is the order of events the same as before? I think the answer to both questions is "No." The main reason for denying the tape recorder analogy of storing meanings is the inherent linearity of a tape recorder. As Schlesinger (1977) argues, there is no left-to-right order in meanings, concepts, or ideas; "such an order is a property only of utterances" (p. 20). Being a cognitively active creature, you are able to shift and modify input and output, and you do not store information in a linear fashion, unless it makes sense to do so.

Semantic Memory

When I talk about the organization of meaning, I am referring to what some scholars call semantic memory. Semantic memory is similar to the semantic organization discussed in Chapter 4 under LTM. Meanings stored in LTM make up your semantic memory.

Cohen (1977) points out that this system of stored meanings is not like a static encyclopedia. It is a working system into which new facts are constantly being added. This implies that your meanings are not fixed, but are changing and growing. As hindsight will tell you, you learn something every time you encounter new experiences. And the more you know about something, the fuller your meaning is about it.

Meanings as Categories

One way to look at meanings is to see them as categories. For instance, you have in your semantic memory a category of "cats." With this category you can identify cats. You can draw a picture of a cat. You can talk about cats. The more you understand cats, the more meaning you have for that category.

Some categories are not so concrete and clear. For instance, your category of "middle-aged" is probably more vague than is your category of "cats." It is considerably harder to see "middle-aged." The cat category is simply more concrete.

Because categories vary in their clarity, people tend to develop what is called the "most typical example" approach to meaning. According to Rosch (1975), you have many examples for each category that you have stored in semantic memory. In order to help clarify each category, you choose one of the examples to be the best representative of that category. To illustrate, let's return to the cats. In your category of cats you have many examples. You have seen different cats. You know what a cat should look like. You know what a cat does. You have feelings about cats. All three of these levels of meaning, though, will be determined by your idea or image of a typical cat. With this typical cat in mind you can assess the "goodness-of-fit" of each cat you encounter. Rosch reminds us that not all cats will meet your standard for the most typical cat. Some will be too fat; others too lazy; still others too wild. By having an ideal type of cat in mind you simplify your category and make it more clear. And the more clear your categories, the more comfortable you are with them.

Having clear categories may be good for your mental health, but it can sometimes lead to differences of opinion between people. A dear friend of mine and I disagree on what a miniature schnauzer dog should look like. His dog has nicely cropped ears that stand erect. My dog has floppy ears, because I didn't feel the need to crop them. My dog doesn't quite meet the standards that my friend has for schnauzers. The point of this story is this. Each of us has an image of a schnauzer. Our images are different, because we are different people. In both cases, our images affected our behavior. My friend had his dog's ears cropped. I didn't. If we would have had similar images, we might have behaved in similar ways. As Rosch's work reminds us, sometimes differences in behavior are caused by differences in images or most typical examples. Since meanings are within people, and since people naturally develop most typical examples, you can expect differences in opinion.

Now that you have an understanding of semantic memory as a category system, let's see how these categories, or meanings, might relate to one another.

Verbal Associations

It is generally agreed that meanings stored in semantic memory are not haphazardly arranged. The system has an internal organization. Just how semantic memory is organized is not well known, but two possibilities are worth noting. The first is a traditional superordinate/subordinate classification system. In other words, meanings can be seen to be stored according to class inclusion. This means that a term like "dog" would be stored under "animal." And "animals" would be stored under "vertebrates." Although this notion seems attractive at first, it doesn't always fit well with the way people use meanings in communication. I rarely talk about dogs as animals. I most often refer to my dogs as pets, and never as vertebrates. Furthermore, I am not too likely to even use a term like "vertebrate" unless I happen to be taking a biology test in which that information would be relevant. Such a traditional view of organizing meaning does not often conform to everyday usage of meaning, nor does it fulfill all three levels of meaning mentioned earlier.

A more appealing alternative to the organization of meanings in LTM comes from verbal *associations*. Verbal associations occur when one word or idea causes you to think of another. This process is similar to cued recall discussed in the last chapter. Meanings are seen as being highly associated when the thought of one leads you to another. Associations can also be responsive to the three levels of meaning. For instance, you can associate a concept like "tennis" with "game" and "ball" (formal). You can associate it with "exercise" (functional). Finally, you can associate tennis with "fun" (affective).

Associations go together because they are learned together. Things that you experience together are likely to be stored together. This is how "salt" is paired with "pepper." And how "black" often leads to "white." Over time, a concept can build up a large family of *associates*. In fact, the more a concept is used in communication the broader its scope of meaning becomes.

Learning Associations

How you have meanings and words associated in your mind is a function of learning. And there are at least two levels of learning that are important to verbal associations. The first is direct experience. That is, I know some things go with other things because I have experienced them that way. At dinner, knives and forks go with plates and glasses; gas and oil go with cars; hammers go with nails. On the other hand, I have learned to associate other things not because of direct experience with them, but because of experience with their usage in language. In fact, most of my associations are formed by observing ideas used in everyday communication. For instance, I know that I can say "The dog ate the bone." But I can't say that "The bone ate the dog." Why? Because bones don't eat dogs. I know that bones don't eat dogs because of two things: (1) my general understanding of the formal, functional, and affective characteristics of bones (my meaning of bones), and (2) the fact that I have never heard anyone talk about bones eating dogs. It is important that you realize that learning takes place when people talk. Bones don't eat dogs because no one has *said* so; therefore I haven't learned it that way.

How people organize their sentences in conversations determines to some degree what others learn about the world by listening to those sentences. You see, language plays an important part in how you have your meanings organized in semantic memory. Your associations (meanings) are not just randomly ordered. They are arranged according to what you know and how you see people talking. Both contribute to your organization of meaning.

Meanings and Natural Language Usage

Researchers don't know just *exactly* how semantic memory is organized. There have been a number of attempts at modeling semantic memory. Researchers such as Anderson and Bower (1973), Rumelhart, Lindsey, and Norman (1972), and Collins and Loftus (1975) propose that semantic memory has two main parts: concepts (or categories, words, etc.) and a set of rules for combining the words into logical and grammatical sentences.

All the popular models of semantic memory conform to two beliefs about the organization of meanings. First is that meanings are learned through association. And these meanings are represented by concepts or categories. The concepts are stored according to the experience that you have watching the "concept in action." Your experience comes primarily through the way people talk about the concepts in every-day conversations. Thus, you learn about meanings through observing them in com-munication. This is called natural language usage.

The second belief is that meanings are organized in such a way to be ready for constructing and understanding sentences. (Read the last sentence again. It is crucial to your understanding of the organization of meaning.) This means that the basic associations that exist between concepts will be governed by rules of language. What this implies is that meanings that rarely appear together in natural language usage (normal conversations) are not likely to be stored together in memory. In other words, the likelihood of two words being associated closely in semantic memory is a function of the likelihood that they are mentioned together in everyday speech. For instance, it would be unlikely to have a concept like "treaty" closely associated in memory to a concept like "wick." On the other hand, it would be quite reasonable to find a category like "game" associated closely with "excitement." Notice that how closely associated two concepts may be in memory is not only a function of their natural "go-togetherness," but it is a function of how often they are made to go together in conversations. Since meanings (concepts) are expressed in communication, they have to be organized in semantic memory in a way that makes them fit natural language usage.

Summary

The organization of meaning is built upon associations between concepts, which provide the "go-togetherness" or the "glue" for semantic memory. Meanings are clusters of associations, but these relationships are governed by natural language usage. Meanings are organized so that we can use them in everyday conversations. Those meanings that are rarely associated in speech are probably not closely associated in semantic memory. Whereas the meaning of a word must include the formal, functional, and affective aspects, the organization of meanings must fit how those meanings are used in everyday speech. Viewing the organization of meaning in this fashion, you are able to preserve the fundamental notion of associations, avoid random organization, and make those associations based on language usage. If you want to know how meanings are organized, listen to how people talk about them.

FORMS OF MEANING

Do meanings have to be verbal? No. Simply because you have a language with which to express your meanings does not assume that meanings themselves are in word form. Cohen (1977) argues that concepts stored in memory are not necessarily verbal. In fact, there are a number of ways that you can represent meanings in your memory. Jerome Bruner (1964) identifies three forms of representation: enactive, iconic, and symbolic. Let's look at each briefly to see how meanings may be repre-sented in these ways.

Enactive representation means that you understand something based on its actions and on your actions toward it. For instance, your understanding of swimming or riding a bicycle is enactively represented in your mind. When you think of riding a bike, you can go through the motions both physically and mentally. *Iconic representa-*

tion deals with your visual images. You have images of many things in your life. Sometimes the mention of a word can call up a number of images. Iconic representation assumes that you can "see" what you are talking about. *Symbolic representation* occurs when you have labeled something. You have a word for your meaning, and you can manipulate the usage of that word through language. This level of representation permits abstractions. In other words, through symbolic representation you can create ideas that probably have no real world referents. For instance, most of us know the word "democracy." But how do you know it when you see it? Your understanding of democracy is created primarily by definition. You can't find one (democracy) at the grocery store. At best, it is a state of affairs; and that state of affairs can best be described symbolically.

Terms like democracy are probably represented at the symbolic level only. Other meanings can be represented at all three levels of representation. For instance, your understanding of "riding a bike" is seated in enactive representation, but you can, no doubt, imagine yourself pedaling down the street. You have an image of bike riding. You should be able to draw a picture of a bike. And you can talk about bike riding. To do these things, you need to have enactive, iconic, and symbolic meanings for bike riding.

What all this comes down to is this. Meanings do not have to be represented in just one way. You can have enactive, iconic, and symbolic meanings about a number of things in your life. Meanings are not just verbal, and they are never definitions.

CREATING MEANING

One of the hazards of studying meanings of words is that you can easily slip back into the myth that words "have" meaning. This can lead you to think that the meaning of a sentence is the sum of the meanings of the words. For instance, if you comprehended that last sentence, you might think it was because you added up the meanings of each of the 21 words and their total produced the meaning of the whole sentence. I hope you didn't do that. To understand what I am writing, you should look for complete thoughts, not for words by themselves. My thoughts are represented in my sentences and clauses. The words are simply vehicles to trigger your already stored meanings. If my phrasing does not provoke the meaning I intend in your mind, I have failed to communicate.

Just as words do not "mean," neither do sentences. I write in sentences because words alone don't work very well. You cannot figure out the meaning of any message by adding up the meanings of the parts of the message. There is simply nothing to add. Only people have meanings. Messages don't.

If messages don't have meaning, then is it possible for an utterance to be meaningful? Yes, it is. What makes an utterance meaningful is that someone intends to communicate something to someone else. Thus, it is the act of communication within a given context that makes a sentence meaningful. In support of this notion, Olson (1970) explains that semantic decisions are not based on the words themselves, but rather on the intended referents that the speaker has in mind. Words are only signals for meaning. The listener must figure out what the speaker means. And the listener gets that from semantic memory. If I choose my signals (words, sentences) appropriately, you should be able to understand what I mean. Hence, determining meaning is a matter of problem-solving. When I communicate to you I am not so much giving you information as I am giving you a problem. If I am able to construct sentences that you are familiar with, I might be able to help you receive my message. But you must do the work of understanding my intended referents.

In essence, then, meaning is created as we communicate. When I talk, you listen and try to create the meaning that I intend. When you talk, I try to form meaning that meets your intentions. In other words, we listen to each other and continually ask—what do you mean? The answer to that running question must come from the receiver. The listener must create the meaning based on the words expressed by the other communicator. As Olson noted, making semantic decisions is a problem-solving task. But it is a problem that we give each other as we talk.

SUMMARY

As I mentioned at the beginning of this chapter, talking about meaning is difficult because meanings are inside your head. I have attempted to give you a better appreciation for meaning by looking at the three levels of meaning (formal, functional, and affective). You also discovered how meanings are organized in semantic memory by associations and how these associations must be responsive to natural language usage. From that point, I demonstrated how meanings can have three different forms (enactive, iconic, and symbolic). Finally, it was re-emphasized that meanings are in people, and not in words. If you want to know what someone means, you must solve the problem by guessing which meanings the words are signaling.

SUMMARY PROPOSITIONS

1. Meanings are a part of the cognitive processes that influence the central system of HIP.
2. Meanings are based on perceptions and are thus personal.
3. Our meanings have at least three levels: formal, functional, and affective.
   a. The formal level has two parts: class inclusion (ISA) and property relations (HASA).
   b. The functional level deals with our understanding of what the intended referent does or what it is used for (DOESA).
   c. The affective level refers to the connotative meanings or feelings and attitudes we have about things.
4. We learn meanings through associations. We acquire associations through direct experience or by listening to concepts being used in everyday conversations.
5. Our meanings are organized according to how they will be used in natural language.
6. Our meanings are not necessarily verbal. They can be represented enactively, iconically, and/or symbolically.
7. We create meaning as we respond to messages. We are continually trying to solve the problem of what the speaker means.

Chapter 6

CENTRALITY OF LANGUAGE
    Language Competence and Performance
COMPETENCE AND COMMUNICATION
NONVERBAL INFORMATION
    Paralanguage and Kinesics
    Nonverbal Memory
    Imagery
LANGUAGE LEARNING
    Hypothesis Testing
    Language Universals
    Four Principles of Language Learning
    Language Learning and HIP
SUMMARY
SUMMARY PROPOSITIONS

Language

The world as you know it today would not be possible without the presence of language. Because of its abstract nature, language opens the door for many activities that are uniquely human. For instance, your ability to communicate is greatly expanded by language. You can talk about things that aren't present, like yesterday. You can negotiate a lease agreement for your new apartment, and you can ask for mustard for your hot dog.

You use language to express yourself and to elicit responses from other people. Language, then, is a social tool through which you interact with others. As anthropologists have observed many times, the sophistication of a society is often dependent on the sophistication of the language spoken in that society. Through language, people learn and develop and so do societies.

Just as the relative sophistication of a society is dependent on its language, so is the relative sophistication of the people using the language. Likewise, your level of thinking (HIP) is partially dependent on your language competence. The more developed your language skills, the more advanced will be your information processing skills. Because language skills help determine your information processing capabilities, you need to understand more about language.

As a topic for a textbook, language is immense. Many excellent books are available that effectively deal with the study of language in human behavior. Since only one chapter is devoted to language here, the coverage will be highly selective and at times very cursory. I will discuss four areas of language: the centrality of language, how language helps you become a competent communicator, how nonverbal information is part of your communication competence, and how language is learned.

CENTRALITY OF LANGUAGE

In this text, my concern with the topic of language centers on your ability to use the rules of language to communicate. Thus, I will not be talking about the traditional elements of language such as phonology and syntax. Rather I will be exploring how language operates to make it easier for you to communicate.

Since language will be viewed as a system of communication rather than a system within itself, let's look at how language, speech, and communication are related conceptually. Figure 6.1 shows a set of concentric circles with language in the center, surrounded by speech, then by communication. This figure shows how language is the core of both speech and communication. Speech is not simply making sounds such as a newborn infant might. Speech is the deliberate manipulation of phonemic sounds for

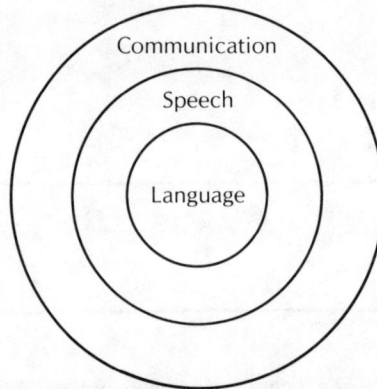

Figure 6.1   The centrality of language in
human communication.

the purpose of communication. Crying, sighing, and other nonlinguistic sounds may communicate, but they are not speech. The outer circle shows that speech and language are systems of communication. It also demonstrates that language and speech are fundamental ingredients of human communication. As you will see later, you can communicate without language and speech (by nonverbal communication), but language and speech are main cogs that make the wheels of communication turn.

Language Competence and Performance

In order to understand your own language abilities, you need to know about two kinds of language skills. *Language competence* refers to your understanding of the rules of language. It means that you know how to put together a grammatically correct sentence. You know the sounds to use (*phonology*), you know how to arrange sentences (*syntax*), and you know how to use words to signal your meaning (*semantics*). All three kinds of knowledge represent your language competence. In essence, your language competence is your knowledge of language.

Language performance is your skill at applying the three kinds of knowledge of language. In other words, your language performance refers to the actual sentences that you say. By observing your sentences, researchers can make judgments about your knowledge of the rules of language (competence). It is assumed that if you produce correct sentences, you have correct understanding of the language rules. Another way to look at this is to call competence "knowledge" and to call performance "behavior." The key thing to realize, though, is that your language behavior is looked upon as evidence of your language knowledge.

Studies that compare language competence with language performance have demonstrated that competence often exceeds performance. In other words, you know how to produce more sentences than you will ever get a chance to say. You also have more meanings than you will ever express. Related to this is the dilemma that you often cannot say what you want to say because your words seem so inadequate. Perhaps you have experienced this when trying to write an important letter or term paper.

As I mentioned earlier, language is a system of communication. You use language to talk about what you know. You also use language to interact with other people.

Language, then, is central to your communication skills. As studies in language competence and performance make clear, your communication skills are dependent on your language skills. The better you are at using and understanding language, the more competently you can communicate. Now let's see how language competence makes you a more competent communicator.

COMPETENCE AND COMMUNICATION

Since your communication skills are dependent on your language competence, then your language competence is part of HIP. Your language competence has a special place in your memory system. Just as you can have memories for meanings, you can have a memory for the rules of language.

I believe that the rules of language are stored in LTM. When your memory for these rules interfaces with your semantic memory for meanings, you can produce and comprehend sentences. What this means is that language competence is stored in memory as an "organizing tool" for encoding (speaking, writing) and decoding (listening, reading) verbal communication. By calling language competence a tool, I am implying that you learn language so you can use it. You do not learn language because language itself is so much fun. You learn language so that you can organize your thoughts for speech. You use your language competence to decipher what someone else is saying to you. If you lived in a society that did not communicate by sentences, you would not need to know about language. Developing language competence, then, is not a natural happening; it is a pragmatic one. If language couldn't help you communicate, it wouldn't be worth bothering with.

Language competence is not innate; it develops because it helps you communicate. Language competence is needed for both comprehension and production of verbal communication. By understanding language, you can produce and understand messages that would otherwise be meaningless to you. If you have ever experienced being part of a fast-moving conversation in a language foreign to you, then you know how linguistic competence (or lack thereof) works to make you part of the conversation or simply an observer of it.

Before going on, let's be careful not to assume that because you do not understand a language that you cannot then communicate. You can. You can always resort to some "semi-universal" gestures that make up the area called nonverbal communication. Those of you who have traveled in foreign countries know that you are not totally lost if you cannot speak the language. Pointing, facial expressions, and tone of voice often communicate enough to keep you out of serious trouble. In fact, nonverbal information interacts so much with verbal communication that you need to know a little more about its supporting role in human communication.

NONVERBAL INFORMATION

So far, I have been talking about competence from a verbal perspective. The verbal skills associated with meanings and language are the mainstays to the cognitive component in the intrapersonal processes. But just as meanings do not have to be verbal, likewise input doesn't have to be verbal. When responding to your world you pay attention to all the information that is available to you, both verbal and nonverbal.

In face-to-face communication, the nonverbal messages are used to support the verbal messages. You use your voice and body to clarify or amplify your verbal messages. And the receiver analyzes these nonverbal messages along with the verbal messages to try to understand your meaning.

Paralanguage and Kinesics

Nonverbal communication occurs through *paralanguage* and *kinesics*. Paralanguage describes your voice characteristics. It refers to *how* you say something, more than to what you say. As you change the loudness, pitch, or timbre of your voice, you are sending nonverbal messages. You can also vary your pausing behavior. You can stop at an unusual point to signal the listener that what you just said was important. You can speed up, slow down, and change your rhythm both to clarify and to amplify your verbal message. Likewise, you can alter your kinesic behavior. Kinesics has been loosely called "body language"; it refers to your gestures, facial expressions, and other body movements that are used in coordination with your spoken words. Just as we can express our meanings with words, we can do it with kinesics as well. Sometime when you are watching TV, turn off the sound and just watch the nonverbal kinesic behavior. You will be surprised how much you can get from seeing without hearing. If the nonverbal messages were not coordinated with the verbal messages, you couldn't make sense out of the action.

Nonverbal Memory

Are nonverbal data stored as part of the cognitive component in the intrapersonal processes of communication? The answer is "Yes." For evidence of this, refer again to Bruner's notions of enactive and iconic representations (Chapter 5). You will recall that enactive representation is your memory for actions, while iconic representation is your visual images. Nonverbal behavior is treated and remembered similarly. As you and I talk face-to-face, both of us record and remember not only what was said but how it sounded and what it looked like. We can remember all three kinds of representation. Thus, nonverbal behavior is just as meaningful as verbal behavior.

Just as you have the rules for language stored in memory, you have the rules for nonverbal communication stored in memory. You know how to gesture when you are making an important point. You know how to show sadness when you are talking about somber matters. You also know how to show excitement when you are making an "exciting" point. People differ in the relative intensity or gusto with which they make nonverbal gestures, but everyone uses nonverbal messages when they communicate. And it is your memory for nonverbal communication that allows you to do so.

Imagery

Nonverbal information plays a significant part in your memory. This is reinforced by Kosslyn (1975), who demonstrated how nonverbal information in the form of images plays a significant part in your ability to recall events. When you recall an event, you can not only remember what was said, you can "see" the scene as well. Using the "mind's eye" you can create an image that matches your prior experience. Suppose your ten-speed bike was stolen and you are at the police station filing a report. No doubt you will be able to describe your missing bicycle. In order to do so, you will call upon your visual memory to form a mental image of it. Your report will include not only the color of the bike, the type of handlebars, etc., but you will be questioned about any unusual marks or scratches on the bike that would help identify it as yours. How well you are able to describe your bike could determine whether it is recovered.

Just as you can recall your stolen bicycle, you can recall the nonverbal aspects of human conversations. People on the witness stand in a courtroom trial are often asked to recall not only what someone said, but also how the other person looked and acted. Most of the time, witnesses can give an account of the nonverbal behavior as well as the verbal behavior. As another illustration, think of the last time you had a face-to-face conversation with your parents. Can't you see them talking with you? You should be able to imagine their faces, whether they were sitting or standing, whether they were happy or sad. As I said earlier, your recall of communication events includes both verbal and nonverbal information. Together they make your recall complete.

One final point. Just as words have more than one meaning, so do many nonverbal behaviors. A wave of the hand can be a sign for hello, goodbye, here I am, I'm next, and so on. As Knapp, Wieman, and Daly (1978) note, you need to examine nonverbal messages as they *co-occur* with verbal behavior in order to know what someone means. Verbal and nonverbal messages go together. They need to be understood in this context.

LANGUAGE LEARNING

There is still some controversy surrounding the acquisition of language, but most researchers agree that language competence and performance need to be developed through learning. In this section, I will look at language learning to show how you got where you are today. But more importantly, you will see how the principles that govern language learning are the same ones that govern information processing and make it expedient.

Without question, the learning of language is one of the most astounding feats of early childhood. By the time you were five years old you were conversing with the language well enough to be sent to school for formal learning. What makes something as complex as language so learnable in a few short years is found in the nature of the learning task itself.

Hypothesis Testing

Language is a rule-based system that is inferred by the learner. As a child, you did not have to experience directly each sentence that you ever said before you said it. In other words, you have uttered many sentences that you have never heard anyone else say before. Even as a little person you did this. How is this possible?

As a child, you witnessed a lot of language in action. You heard others talking. From this corpus of language behavior you were able to make inferences about the rules underlying the sentences you heard. For instance, if a child hears a parent say to another child, "Hector, please come inside," he or she learns not only the words but also how to put together a command. Furthermore, the child will focus not just on the words but on the voice, the body action, the situation, and on Hector's reaction. Experiencing all this, the child then creates hypotheses about the underlying rules and then tries them out on someone else later. It is not necessary for the child to directly imitate what he or she heard before. The child must simply try to form a command using what he or she believes to be the proper rules for producing such a remark. Direct imitation of others plays a lesser part in language learning than was once believed. Insup Taylor (1976) reminds us that "with our limited memory capacity, it is more sensible for us to acquire a vocabulary and a set of rules that we can apply to new utterances, than to try to memorize all possible utterances" (p. 190).

To get a proper picture of how you learned language, you must see yourself as an active processor of information. Even today you are actively observing language and forming hypotheses about the language. By doing this you can create sentences that you have never uttered before. Those attempts at language performance that are socially reinforced are retained by you. Those that are not reinforced positively are subject to rejection by you. Over time, you have built your language competence by testing your linguistic performance. When you make a mistake in speech, you must learn not only to avoid the error in the future, you must alter your prior hypothesis that produced the incorrect utterance.

Language Universals

One of the research findings that has led current thinking to the more active, generative model of language learning (in place of the imitation model) is the work in language *universals*. By comparing the language development process of children from different cultures (with different languages), researchers have discovered a set of language universals indicating that language development follows a strikingly similar pattern across cultures. Language universals, then, are the common principles of language that all learners follow regardless of the language they are learning. Dan Slobin (1979) has compiled a list of strategies or operating principles that summarize how children acquire language. If you are interested and willing to cope with some linguistic terminology often unfamiliar to the beginning reader, you should consult Slobin's work listed in the references for this chapter. For my purpose here, I simply want to leave you with the impression that researchers are moving closer and closer to a complete understanding of the universal characteristics of language that allow the child to acquire language in an orderly and expedient fashion.

Four Principles of Language Learning

Of all the language universals that have been discovered, four are especially relevant to an information-processing approach to language. These four principles apply to all normal children, and as you will see, adults as well.

First, one of the more consistent patterns of language acquisition is that *development proceeds from the simple to the more complex*. For instance, children often acquire vowels before they master many consonants. Even initial syntax is simplified. The child's grammar starts out holophrastic (one word representing a whole sentence) before growing into two to three words (telegraphic speech). Another example of simplification is the way in which young children negate sentences. Before learning to say "can't" and "don't" in the middle of sentences, children first negate sentences by simply placing "no" at the beginning. For example, younger children are more likely to say "No want to go home," rather than "I don't want to go home." Since placing "no" at the beginning is easier than modifying the verb, younger children choose this strategy before learning the other more complex option. Language learning goes from the simple to the complex.

A second standard pattern in language acquisition is *overgeneralization*. Often when children discover a rule of language they will overuse it. The most common example of this is placing an "-ed" ending on verbs to make them past tense. Consequently, children are likely to say something such as "We eated dinner," or "He comed here." In order to overcome this problem, children must learn that not all verbs can be made into the past tense by adding "-ed," then they must learn which verbs (like the ones above) need special treatment.

Overgeneralization is hardly an irrational act. If you think about it, our language is more inconsistent than is the child trying to learn it. If a child were learning Spanish, for example, this particular problem of overgeneralization would be eliminated. Because the English language has so many exceptions to basic grammatical rules, overgeneralization is bound to occur.

Third, *our receptive capabilities often exceed our expressive capabilities*. This is especially true in language development. Children seem to understand more than they can say. In a series of tests comparing children's abilities to imitate, comprehend, and produce sentences, Fraser, Bellugi, and Brown (1963) presented three-year-olds with pictures and asked them questions about the pictures (comprehension test). They were also asked to create a sentence describing the picture (production test). What the researchers found was that the children were far more able to comprehend sentences (questions) about the pictures than they were to produce sentences describing the pictures. In other words, their receptive skills outperformed their production skills. (They also found that children's ability to imitate sentences exceeded both comprehension and production.)

The problem of knowing more than you can say is easy to observe in young children's talk. You may have noticed that little children seem to take forever to tell a story or recall an event. They start the story, get mixed up, and then go back and start all over again. Sometimes a simple event comes out as a jumbled mass of confusion. As you listen to such a story, you know that the child has something definite in mind, but just can't get it out smoothly. Yet these same children can sit down and listen to a story with many details without losing track of what is happening in the story. Because they seem to listen and comprehend better than they speak, researchers conclude that their receptive skills are better than their expressive skills.

Fourth, perhaps the most important universal language learning pattern is that people *pay attention to the whole communication act* when learning language, not just to speech alone. Shatz (1978) conducted two studies that demonstrated that children understand utterances in reference to the action(s) going on at the time. Children listen to the speech behavior, but they are also aware of the context. Furthermore, children realize at a very young age that meaning must be derived from the surrounding action as well as from the speech. Given this, one might argue that language without a speaker, actions, and a context would not be very meaningful and thus not worth bothering with. Children learn language not because language is interesting, but because of what happens when language is being performed.

Language Learning and HIP

Although there are more principles that affect the language learning process, the four mentioned here are included because they relate easily to how adults process information through language. For instance, like children, adults tend to learn in a simple-to-complex pattern. The more you are exposed to something, the more you can analyze it for more intricate details. Going to a movie a second time often reveals things you missed the first time. The more you experience something the more deeply you can process it. Professional photographers look at photographs with a much more critical eye than do Grandma and Grandpa at Christmas. What about the second principle of overgeneralization? Do adults overgeneralize? Do you learn something and then apply it as often as you can even though it doesn't fit every circumstance? Adult problem-solving is often overgeneralized. When faced with a problem that is similar to one you've faced before, you apply the same solution you used in the past even though another one would be better. As far as the third principle goes, research indicates that adult receptive skills are larger than adult expressive skills. All of us, at one time or another, have had difficulty expressing ourselves. Adult vocabulary size varies, depending on whether you are reading, writing, or speaking. Your reading vocabulary (receptive) is the largest, while your speaking vocabulary (expressive) is the smallest. As you will see in a later chapter, your speaking style is considerably simpler than your reading style. Finally, consider how you interpret other people as they are talking with you. Don't you attend to everything that is going on? If you are like most adults, you pay attention to the words and to the paralanguage and kinesics. You are also aware of the context. You know what is going on.

You see, many principles that make language learning expedient are the same ones that make HIP expedient. Processing language is a form of processing information. As humans, you and I are not born with language, but we are probably born with capabilities for HIP, out of which come things such as language learning.

SUMMARY

Language is a system of communication. Its attractiveness comes from its social utility. Through language you can do things animals cannot. Your understanding or knowledge of the rules of language is your competence. Your linguisitc competence helps you both generate and decipher language performance. Thus, your knowledge of language serves as an organizing tool so you can express and understand meanings. You are also competent in handling nonverbal information. Your competence at language and at nonverbal information processing together make you a competent communicator.

Finally, you have seen how language is acquired in a very learner-oriented, active manner. The child infers the rules of language from watching language in action. Language development follows a well-organized, predictable set of principles designed to make learning simple and expedient. Children around the world seem to learn language in similar ways regardless of the language they are learning. Because language is a part of HIP, its development affects the child's information processing skills. Children don't reason in the complex ways that adults do, and this is clearly evidenced in their communication behavior. The more proficient people are in their language skills, the more proficient they will be at information processing. You cannot separate language skills from the more general skills of HIP.

SUMMARY PROPOSITIONS

1. Language is a system of communication.
2. Speech is spoken language, not just producing sounds.

3. The core of communication behavior is language.

4. Language competence is knowledge of the rules of language.

5. Language performance is how you apply your understanding of the rules of language to produce actual sentences.

6. Language competence is stored in memory and is an organizing tool for encoding and decoding sentences.

7. Part of your communication competence is your ability to interpret nonverbal information.

8. You have memories for nonverbal information just as you have memories for meanings and language.

9. Language learning takes place in an efficient and orderly fashion. It is characterized by the following patterns:

   a. Development proceeds from the simple to the complex.

   b. We overgeneralize our understanding of specific language rules.

   c. Our receptive capabilities often exceed our expressive capabilities.

   d. People pay attention to the whole communication act when learning language.

10. As you become more proficient in using your language and building your meanings, you can process more information more quickly and more thoroughly.

4 AFFECTIVE COMPONENT

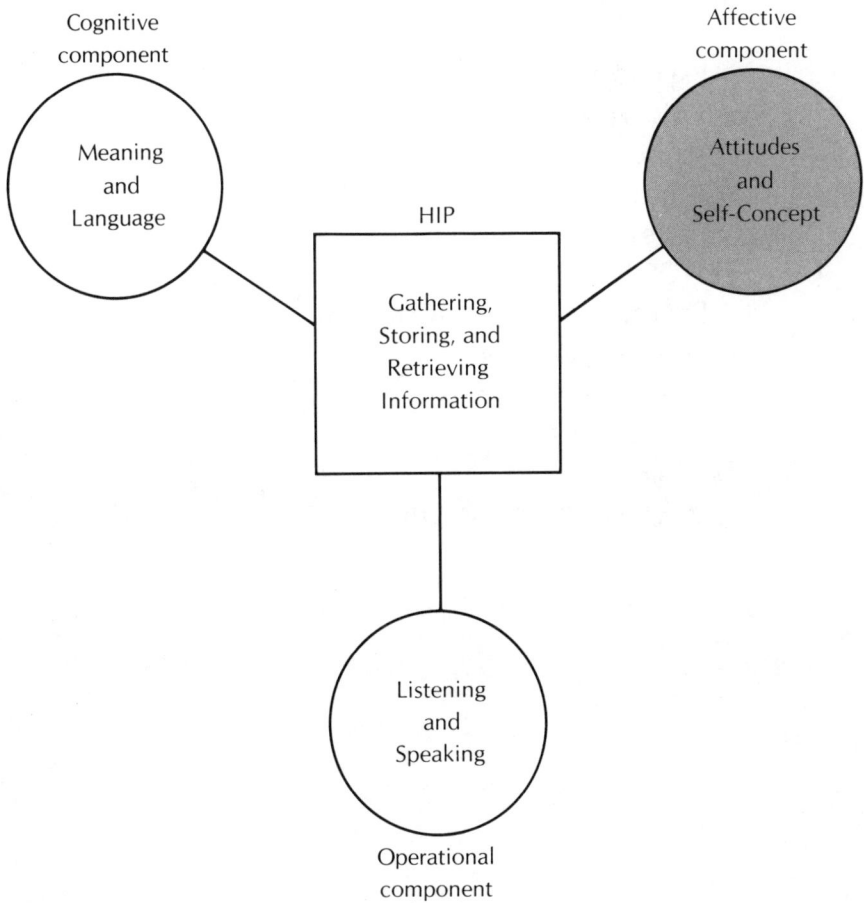

Cognitive
component

Affective
component

Meaning
and
Language

Attitudes
and
Self-Concept

HIP

Gathering,
Storing, and
Retrieving
Information

Listening
and
Speaking

Operational
component

Chapter 7

CONSISTENCY
    Striving for Consistency
    Psycho-Logic
VAB SYSTEM
    Values
    Attitudes
    Beliefs
SELF-CONCEPT
    Learning Your Self-Concept
    Low Self-Concept
    Cognitive Complexity
    Some Risks
SUMMARY
SUMMARY PROPOSITIONS

Attitudes and Self-Concept

It would be tempting to describe human information processing as a simple data processing system wherein people gather, store, and retrieve information without error. Such, however, is simply not the case. When people handle information, they personally distort it. It is not enough, though, to say that people distort information. You need to know why they do it. You need to explore how information gets "personalized."

It is my belief that the affective component (attitudes and self-concept) contributes greatly to information distortion in HIP. If you and I did not have attitudes and self-concepts, we might be able to handle information unemotionally. But as Bugelski (1973) reminds us, "We cannot dichotomize behavior into the emotional and nonemotional. There is no time in our lives when we are free of emotional influences" (p. 437).

As you take in information it is not only deciphered through your language competence and given meaning by semantic memory, it is also filtered through your feelings. In Chapter 5, I proposed three levels of understanding that are applied as you assign meaning to a message. At level three the question was, "How do I feel about this?" Thus in your effort to grasp meaning you make subjective decisions as well as objective ones. Because of the emotional subjectivity of HIP, you need to consider attitudes and self-concepts. If Bugelski is correct, you need to have at least a passing understanding of the affective component of the intrapersonal processes of communication.

This chapter is divided into three parts. The first section is on consistency. I believe that the main organizing principle of the affective component is consistency, which governs your attitudes and self-concept. The next section looks at the values—attitudes—beliefs (*VAB*) system. All three work together to determine your feelings about messages. Finally, I will demonstrate how your self-concept affects your communication and your information processing abilities.

CONSISTENCY

For reasons that are not clearly understood, people seem to expect consistency in their thoughts and actions. It is assumed that a person's observable behavior serves as an accurate thermometer of internal feelings. People who are angry should act angry. People who are happy should act happy. Yet, sometimes external behaviors are inconsistent with internal feelings. For instance, how a person actually votes in an election may be entirely different from what that person told the boss at work earlier that day. When your actions don't agree with your feelings you are being inconsistent. Since this is considered undesirable, most people try to avoid inconsistency.

67

Striving for Consistency

Just as your body functions to maintain *homeostasis* (balance) for "good health," your mind appears to strive for the same balance psychologically. People like to have their feelings coincide with their experiences. They like to believe that they have their "heads in order" most of the time. Psychological disorder is stressful.

This basic belief has produced three assumptions about the affective component of HIP:

1. People have a need for consistency. (It is a preferred state.)

2. Inconsistency is drive producing. (The stress produces a desire to do something about the inconsistency.)

3. Inconsistency must be reconciled. (You must reach some resolution even if you "rationalize" your problem.)

If this model of consistency is accurate, then you would expect people to work for consistency. You would also expect people to avoid situations that throw them into the stress of inconsistency. Although striving for consistency and avoiding inconsistency are generally preferred, you will see in the next chapter that there are exceptions to avoiding inconsistency.

Psycho-Logic

Because people strive for consistency, they take incoming information and make it fit what they already know. This occurs even if it means distorting the incoming information to make it fit better. Through selective perception you are able to fit the new information with your current understanding.

Sometimes the fitting of new information into old information calls for some fancy intellectual footwork to avoid appearing illogical. For instance, your friends might know you as a "true" Democrat. Yet in the last election, you voted for another party's candidate. Were you illogical? It depends. If you voted that way because you accidentally switched the wrong lever on the voting machine, you made a simple mistake. On the other hand, your choice may have been quite deliberate, but to your friends it appears contradictory. How do you justify this apparent inconsistency? If inconsistency is stressful, you certainly didn't vote for the other candidate to bring stress into your life.

The answer to the above problem lies in the logic that underlies your values, attitudes, and beliefs. It would be nice if people were logical in the sense that philosophers of logic talk about, but they are not. The logic of your feelings follows a *psycho-logic* rather than a formal logic. When questioned by your friends for your voting behavior, you should be able to conjure up reasons that justify your behavior. They may not accept your reasons, but if the reasons make sense to you, that's what matters. Regardless of what others think, your feelings and behaviors do not have to meet the standards of formal logic. To my knowledge, no one has ever been logical in every decision.

The principle of consistency is a personal matter; it is a case of personal perception. As long as your beliefs and actions do not conflict with those of most of your friends, you can maintain your own psychological structure. In reality, no one is consistent or inconsistent. People are consistent or inconsistent only when someone says they are. It is similar to baseball umpires arguing over whether a pitcher commits a balk. After squabbling over the details that make certain moves on the mound an infraction of the rule, one umpire concludes in frustration, "It ain't anything, 'til I call it a balk!" Likewise, you cannot know *in fact* when someone is being consistent or inconsistent.

In striving for consistency, then, you use a psycho-logic that allows you to incorporate new information with old information. This same psycho-logic also permits you to justify your behavior when it seems to be inconsistent with known values, attitudes, and beliefs.

VAB SYSTEM

Your internalized feelings about a topic are called your values, attitudes, and beliefs (VAB). They make up the part of the affective component that I have been calling *attitudes*, but a more complete understanding requires considering values and beliefs in addition to attitudes. Figure 7.1 shows how the three are interrelated.

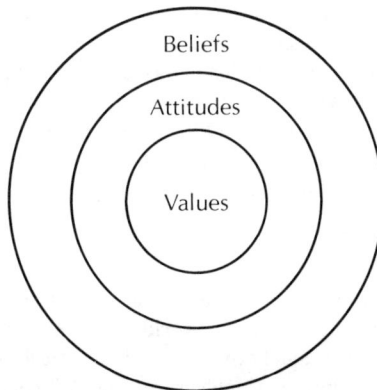

Figure 7.1   The interrelationships of the VAB system.

Values

At the very center of your feelings are your values. Your values are those feelings that you hold "near and dear" to you. They are your main standards of life. They are deep-seated, difficult to change, and firmly associated with your personal identity. Values include such things as honesty, cleanliness, and fair play. Rokeach (1968) suggests that you have many attitudes but few values. His value survey test, used nationwide, consists of two parts, each listing only 18 values. According to Rokeach, these are the most prominent values in America. McCroskey and Wheeless (1976) argue that although people have a limited number of values, they "form the basis for most of our behavioral habits" (p. 127). These long-enduring feelings seem to be, then, your standards or basic evaluations that are applicable throughout your life. Because they do not change easily, they serve as solid anchors for your decisions in life. Finally, these values determine the attitudes and beliefs that you can consistently hold.

Attitudes and beliefs that contradict your personal value system tend to meet strong resistance from you. People simply find it difficult to hold attitudes and beliefs that clash with their values.

Attitudes

In between values and beliefs in Figure 7.1 are your attitudes. Attitudes are traditionally defined as your predisposition to respond positively or negatively to ideas, people, or objects. Whereas values are evaluations that apply to many instances, attitudes are object-specific. By that I mean that you have a specific attitude for each object of evaluation. Your attitudes represent how much you like or dislike something. Your judgment about whether something is good or bad comes from your attitude about it. When you publicly express your attitudes you are giving your opinions. Opinions, then, are your verbalized attitudes.

Attitude change is the goal of persuasion. Attitudes are subject to change more often than are values. A speech can change your attitude, but it is less likely to change your value system. Whether an attitude will change depends on its strength. The more extreme one's attitude is toward a topic, the more difficult it will be to change that attitude. On the other hand, weak, apathetic attitudes are much easier to change. Having an apathetic neutral position on an issue can make you very susceptible to persuasion. Because of this, some people develop attitude positions that are sufficiently strong to give them some resistance to attempts to change their minds. So, if you have a relative or friend who seems "locked into his/her point of view," that kind of narrow-mindedness may be for defensive purposes. Most people don't like to change their point of view very often. It is too much work, and it could lead to confusion for those who are constantly re-evaluating their attitudes.

Beliefs

Surrounding your attitudes and values are your beliefs. Your beliefs are your perceptions about the "real" world. They are observations that you think are true. They are not necessarily evaluative like attitudes and values. Rather they vary on a true–false continuum (McCroskey and Wheeless 1976). For instance, you might believe that the chair you are sitting in will continue to support you as you read this book. Or you might believe that the sun will rise tomorrow. You might even believe that most people are well intending, but they just make mistakes once in a while. These are beliefs. They are matters of faith. The key to beliefs is that you think they are true. Whether they really are is often debatable.

Like attitudes and values, beliefs are important to you. Some of your beliefs are more important than others, such as religious beliefs, beliefs about your own abilities, and beliefs about the sincerity of your friends. The more important the belief, the more resistant to change that belief will be. I could do quite well persuading you about matters that you don't see as important. But if we disagree upon a topic that you believe in strongly and hold intense attitudes about, my persuasive messages may fail.

Your values, attitudes, and beliefs work together to help you filter incoming information. Your feelings determine, in part, how susceptible you will be to persuasion. Strong values, attitudes, and beliefs form strong barriers to persuasive messages. Part of the reason for this is in the interconnection of your values, attitudes, and beliefs. The three parts of the VAB system tend to exist in harmony with each other.

They fit together. They support each other. For instance, let's say that you recently purchased a life insurance policy. When asked about your decision by one of your friends, you might justify your action with statements similar to these:

"It is important to protect your family" (value).

"The policy I bought is one of the best on the market" (attitude).

"I bought from a man who gave me straight talk, no heavy sales pitches" (belief).

There are many other possible statements that could fit into these, but the important thing to note is that if you changed any of the above three statements into its opposite, you would have an inconsistent set of values, attitudes, and beliefs. If this inconsistency is sufficiently strong to create a drive state, you would have to find a way to reconcile yourself. But as long as you can keep these three elements together, you will be happy with your decision.

SELF-CONCEPT

So far, I have talked about how people prefer consistency in their values, attitudes, and beliefs. You saw how values, attitudes, and beliefs are organized in a supportive manner with each other. You also discovered that the vulnerability of the VAB system is dependent on the importance of the subject at hand. There is another concept in the affective component that needs to be introduced here. It, too, affects your vulnerability to incoming information. It also affects your style of handling information. It is your self-concept.

Your self-concept is a major part of your quest for consistency. As Rosenberg (1968) remarked, "The need for . . . the maintenance of internally consistent affective–cognitive structures is often subordinated to man's penchant for trying to think well of himself and optimistically of his prospects" (p. 384). How you see yourself, in part, affects how you process information and communicate with other people. Furthermore, you know yourself by observing the roles you play in life and the attributes you see yourself as having. This collection of roles and attributes constitutes your self-concept.

Let me illustrate how your self-concept is derived from your perceived roles and attributes. If I asked you, "Who are you?", you would probably list items such as your name, your occupation, hobbies, and physical features. I remember a student who described himself in front of class as a "Baptist, outstanding softball player, ERA advocate, conservationist, and philatelist." After checking my pocket dictionary for the social propriety of the last term (stamp collector) I pointed out to the class how his list consisted of roles and attributes that described his values, attitudes, and beliefs. People often define themselves in terms of roles and attributes; but more than that, self-concepts are typically structured around their VAB system. How people define themselves often tells you about how they view themselves and the world around them. When you get to know someone's self-concept, you get to know that person's VAB system.

Learning Your Self-Concept

Where do you get your self-concept? Is it like your inborn personality? The answer is "No." Your self-concept is how you see *you as a person*. It is your attitude about you. Your personality provides some of the data for your judgments about yourself, but your self-concept is separate from your personality. Your self-concept emerges from social interaction. You learn who you are from observing yourself and observing how other people react to you. If you think that you are a good dancer, it is because you've been told so. If you believe you are a good chess player, it is because you have beat at least one other person who plays chess, or you have been told by someone you respect that you are a good chess player. You discover who you are by social interaction. Without others, you cannot develop a self-concept.

Feedback from others, then, contributes heavily to your understanding of your self. Any significant interaction with someone else can have one or more of the following effects on your self-concept:

1. It can *add* to your self-concept. (It can make you see yourself in a new light.)

2. It can *clarify* your self-concept. (You can more accurately understand your roles and attributes.)

3. It can *cause doubt* about your self-concept. (A conversation can cause you to question your own abilities.)

4. It can *cause major changes* in your self-concept. (You re-evaluate your self and undergo a significant change in your opinion of yourself.)

I'm sure that a number of you have experienced one or more of the above changes in self-concept. It is amazing how you may feel one way about yourself at one minute, then someone says something to cause you to reconsider your previous opinions of yourself. It is easy to overlook the way in which a remark can have a significant impact on someone's life.

Research has shown that negative feedback can reduce a person's self-concept. On the other hand, positive feedback reinforces and enhances one's self-concept (Maehr, Mensing, and Nafzgher 1962). It has also been discovered that people tend to affiliate themselves with other people who reinforce their adopted self-concepts (Berscheid and Walster 1969). Apparently, people are not comfortable with other people who "put them down." Rather, people prefer others who "lift them up."

Low Self-Concept

You can imagine what effect a low self-concept could have on your information processing skills and your communication behavior. People who are unsure of themselves have low self-concepts and could become quite introverted. McCroskey and Wheeless (1976) note that "people with low self-esteem lack confidence in their own ability . . . and tend to accept other people's views readily because they consider their own views to be of less value . . ." (pp. 130–31). Goss, Olds, and Thompson (1978) found a strong correlation between one's self-esteem and level of communication apprehension. People with high communication apprehension (stage fright) tend to have low self-concepts. Thus, the more unsure you are about yourself, the more susceptible to influence you will be, and the more "uptight" you will be about your ability to express yourself.

Another effect of a low self-concept is called the "self-fulfilling prophecy." When applied to self-concepts, the self-fulfilling prophecy suggests that when people are given labels that supposedly describe them, they behave according to the label. Calling someone "lazy" increases the chances that the person will act lazy. Calling someone a "poor public speaker" makes that person a poor public speaker. If you have "never been good at math," you might have more trouble with your statistics class than those who have never declared a deficiency in math. Oddly enough, you can even attribute a self-concept to someone before ever meeting that person for the first time. If someone during the first day of class tells you "This professor is always late to class, and boring once he gets here," that should increase the likelihood that you will look for things that confirm this ascribed image. Even our colleges and universities have labeling problems related to self-concepts. For instance, your college may have special programs for "honors" students or a program for "threshold" students. To some degree, the relative performance of students in such programs is predetermined by labeling them so. Both the teachers and the students know why they are in the program. And knowledge of how things *should* turn out helps them to turn out that way.

Sometimes people with low self-concepts wish that they were "somebody else." In other words, they dislike their current self-concept and aspire to another one. This is called an aspired self-concept. It is the image of the self that a person wishes to be someday. An aspired self-concept may be beneficial for personal motivation and self-improvement, but it can also cause problems since it may imply that you do not like who you are. Not liking yourself is bad enough, but what can follow is worse. People who aspire to something they are not can develop habits of deception. Such habits, in turn, can affect how they communicate. By wanting to be someone they are not, they may lie to people or exaggerate a lot. People who frequently lie and exaggerate may be unsure of themselves and of their ideas. This kind of behavior may be found in job interviews. An applicant who is unsure of his or her qualifications might stretch a point or two and even lie about something that may be interpreted as undesirable. Obviously, no one wants to get caught in a lie. So it is better to accept yourself as you are, and tell the truth.

Cognitive Complexity

Part of your self-concept is the way in which you view your ability to process information. Some people can handle a lot of information at one time. They can make sense out of it and not feel serious frustration. Others say that they could never do that.

How you judge your ability to cope with information is related to what is called *cognitive complexity*. People who are high in cognitive complexity are able to take in a lot of information at one time and make sense out of it. They do not get overloaded very easily. Those who overload easily are low in cognitive complexity. I have already established the fact that people with low self-concepts do not cope with information very well. Low self-concept people will probably be low in cognitive complexity as well.

How do you see yourself in terms of cognitive complexity? Can you sort through a lot of details and make sense out of them? Or do you prefer to have things spelled out, step-by-step? In terms of communication, research shows that the more cognitive complexity you have, the more skilled you will be in communication interactions with other people (Saine 1976). You will be able to make more sense out of what is said. Your cognitive complexity may even manifest itself in your style of speaking and writing, but better measures of complexity and style are needed before we can have complete confidence in this relationship (Powers, Jordan, and Street 1979).

No matter how you feel about yourself or your cognitive complexity, other people will eventually notice these things about you. Your self-concept shows in how you process information and in how you communicate. To present a good self-concept, you must accept who you are, then let your acceptance show. There is nothing better for your "mental health" than a healthy self-concept. And a healthy self-concept depends on personal self-acceptance.

Some Risks

As I said earlier, you learn your self-concept by observing how others react to you. Likewise, your self-concept can be tested through your interactions with other people. If you believe that you are good at your job but want to "know for sure," should you run the risk of publicly displaying your work for evaluation? Should you ask others their opinions of your work? This can be risky, and you must be ready for the consequences. As Burgoon and Ruffner (1978) ask, "Is it better to seek out . . . confirmation of the self and possibly risk finding out that you are not who you think you are, or is it better to play it safe and avoid instances where disconfirmation is likely?" (p. 465). Your choice will probably depend on the "health" of your self-concept. If you are sure about yourself, you might take the chance. If you are unsure about yourself, you may hold back and play it safe. Unfortunately, some people choose the latter option more than they should. How about you?

SUMMARY

Information processing is not a simple data-in, data-out process. The affective component "colors" how you deal with information. How you receive and retrieve information is affected by your values, attitudes, and beliefs and by your self-concept. When you assign meanings to messages you do so with your feelings in mind. These affective elements play a large part in how you speak and listen.

The underlying principle of the affective component is consistency. You organize your VAB system and your self-concept so they can exist together in harmony. In order to maintain psychological balance, you employ a psycho-logic that permits you to justify your feelings and actions. If you find yourself in an inconsistent situation, you will find ways to resolve it, even if it means that you simply rationalize your behaviors.

In this chapter, you discovered how your attitudes are supported by your foundational values and surrounding beliefs. All three fit together to provide a rationale for your actions. You also discovered how people differ in their self-concepts and in their cognitive complexity. A low self-concept can be detrimental to information processing skills. A healthy view of yourself will acknowledge your uniqueness and will be girded up by your own self-acceptance.

SUMMARY PROPOSITIONS

1. HIP is subjective as well as objective.
2. The main organizing principle for the affective component is consistency.
3. A homeostatic point of view assumes:
   a. People have a need for consistency.
   b. Inconsistency is drive producing.
   c. Inconsistency must be reconciled.
4. Consistency assumes a psycho-logic as opposed to a formal logic.
5. Your internalized feelings are called values, attitudes, and beliefs (VAB system).
   a. Values represent your innermost standards for life.
   b. Attitudes are how you feel about ideas, people, or objects.
   c. Beliefs are observations that you think are true.
6. Your self-concept is your attitude about you as a person.
7. You learn your self-concept by observing yourself and observing how people react to you.
8. A low self-concept affects how you process information and how you communicate.
9. How you feel about yourself is dependent on how much you can accept yourself as you are.

Chapter 8

BALANCE
  P–O–X Triangles
  Preference for Balance
  Unit Relationship
  Timing
CONGRUITY
  Applications to HIP
COGNITIVE DISSONANCE
  Justification
  Postdecisional Dissonance
  Selective Exposure
  Resolving Inconsistency
  Applications to HIP
SUMMARY
SUMMARY PROPOSITIONS

Consistency Theories

In the last chapter, I introduced the concept of consistency. I argued that consistency is the governing principle by which you organized your feelings. The affective component of the intrapersonal processes of communication is maintained through consistency.

Over the past 30 years or so, a number of attitude-change theories have emerged that are based on the assumption that people strive to keep their attitudes consistent with each other. The most often cited consistency theories are the *balance theory* of Heider (1946), Osgood and Tannenbaum's (1955) *congruity theory*, and Festinger's (1957) *dissonance theory*. As the dates in the references suggest, these theories developed from each other. Each theory is grounded in the belief that inconsistency produces stress that must be reconciled if the person is to maintain a homeostatic state. Since these theories have received such widespread recognition in academic circles, and since they are relevant to an information processing approach to communication, each will be considered separately.

BALANCE

In 1946, and later in 1958, Fritz Heider spelled out his theory of interpersonal balance. This theory became the backbone of much of the research in persuasion. But it also applies to how you keep your feelings together in your mind. Thus it is relevant to HIP.

The theory is really quite simple. It has three essential elements: two people and a topic of conversation. Heider proposes that the two people will be working to keep their relationship harmonious while holding consistent attitudes about the topic of conversation. Let's look more closely at this situation.

P−O−X Triangles

Heider proposes a P−O−X triangle model for describing two people talking about a topic (Figure 8.1). P represents you, O is the other person you are talking with, and X is the topic at hand.

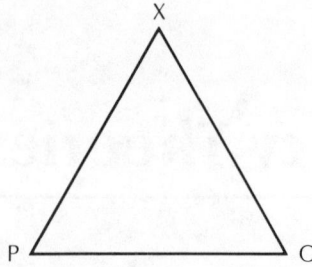

Figure 8.1   The P-O-X triangle model of
Heider's (1946, 1958) balance
theory.

On any of the three lines connecting the elements (P, O, X) is either a positive (+) or a
negative (−) sign indicating a positive or negative relationship between the elements.
For instance, in Figure 8.2, you (P) like me (O), and you like classical music (X).
Similarly, I like classical music. This triadic relationship is balanced.

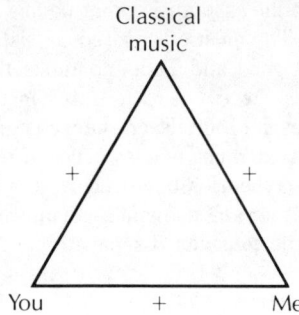

Figure 8.2   A balanced P-O-X triangle.

If one of the positive signs were changed to a negative sign, the situation would be
unbalanced. Hence, if I didn't like classical music (negative sign), you would probably
not invite me to your place to listen to Beethoven's Ninth Symphony. It would be
inconsistent for you to do so. But as long as we don't have to relate to each other very
often about classical music, this unbalanced state can be avoided by mutual agreement. Choosing to avoid unbalanced situations is a common strategy used by people
who wish to keep away from possible stress in life. More will be said about coping with
unbalanced situations later.

How about a situation wherein P and O dislike each other? As Figure 8.3
demonstrates, example *a* is balanced, because people whom you dislike are also likely
to disagree with you on a number of topics. Therefore, it is consistent to expect such a
person to disagree with you. You should feel no particular stress from this situation.
On the other hand, when someone you dislike agrees with you on a topic, as in example
b, this can be irritating. Example *b* can be quickly translated into the "eternal
triangle" problem, when two people fall in love with the same person and thus come to
hate each other.

If you were to lay out all the possible triangles using this approach, you would find
eight—four balanced, four unbalanced. A convenient way to test the balance—
unbalance outcome of each triangle is to multiply the signs. If the product is positive,
the triangle is balanced. If the product is negative, it is unbalanced.

X

+   −

P   −   O

a

X

+   +

P   −   O

b

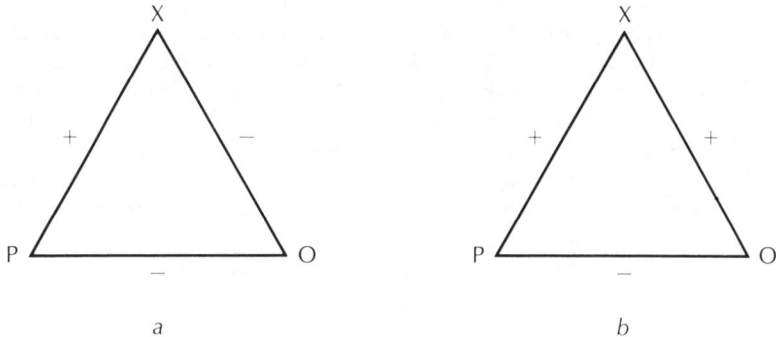

Figure 8.3   The P-O-X triangles:
a, balanced; *b*, unbalanced.

It is important to note that X can be an object, person, place, or idea. As long as two people have an attitude about it, either positive or negative, it can be a topic of discussion (or in some cases, a bone of contention).

Preference for Balance

The situations depicted by the P−O−X triangles are more than "academic." According to research, people are able to relate quite easily to the situations described by the triangles. Furthermore, research shows that people have very definite preferences for balanced situations over unbalanced ones. Jordan (1953) asked subjects to rate the "pleasantness" of 64 different hypothetical social situations. Each situation reflected one of the triangles. As expected, they tended to rate the balanced situations as more pleasant than the unbalanced ones. Feather (1967) found similar results in his work.

The preference for balance may also affect your memory. Zajonc (1968) found that balanced situations were easier to store and remember than were unbalanced ones. People recalled a greater number of pleasant memories than they did unpleasant ones. I know I can more readily recall "good times" than other "not-so-good times" from my childhood. The bad times seem to be suppressed in memory. Good memories are just more fun to remember.

Unit Relationship

On the surface, it appears as though balance theory works with only likes and dislikes. Actually, there is a little more to it than that. The relative impact of any of the likes (+) and the dislikes (−) in the triangles is a function of the importance of the underlying relationships. For instance, if a well-known football player is shown endorsing a certain brand of boots in a magazine ad, it will have little effect on my attitude toward the boots, because although I may like the football player, I have no compelling relationship with him. If I don't buy the boots, he'll never know about it. Even if I sneeze all over the magazine ad, he'll never know. You see, the athlete and I are not in any kind of *unit relationship*.

A unit relationship occurs when two people or ideas seem to go together regularly. My wife and I have a unit relationship. I have unit relationships with my colleagues at work. When the plumber comes to fix my sewer lines, we enter into a unit relationship (he does the work, I pay him). A unit relationship assumes that two people can mutually affect one another. A football player in a magazine cannot affect me. Therefore, I can resist the persuasive message without much effort.

Unit relationships are important to balance theory, because without them the theory wouldn't work very well. Let me illustrate. You might be faced by two people. One you care for very much and enjoy being with regularly. The other person may be a stranger whom you know very little about and don't plan on seeing again except by accident. Which one of these two people would have more impact on you in a P–O–X situation? Certainly the former person would be more influential than the latter one. Balance theory works, but only when you are in a unit relationship with the other person. This is the main reason that celebrity endorsement of products often fails. Unless the respondent feels particularly "close" to the celebrity (hero worship?), the endorsement will have minimal impact.

Timing

The effectiveness of balance theory also depends on timing. Immediacy is the key word here. If you are faced with an immediate problem and someone says something that calls for a decision on your part, you will be susceptible to the principles of balance. For instance, if you just admitted a loved one to the hospital and the physician informs you that immediate surgery is needed, you are likely to agree with the doctor even if you hate surgery and cannot afford its cost. But if you are watching TV and a person wearing physician's clothes recommends a liquid for upset stomachs, your vulnerability to that ad will be a function of whether you have a stomachache. If you don't have any stomach pain, you can ignore the ad; but if the ad comes on at a time when your stomach is aching, the ad may persuade you. The impact of persuasive messages depends on their timing. People who do not have an immediate need for a product will not try to balance their lives by buying the product.

CONGRUITY

In 1955, Osgood and Tannenbaum made some changes to improve the predictability of Heider's balance theory. Their modifications centered on scaling the liking/ disliking scores. Instead of the simple + or − sign between the elements in the P–O–X triangles, Osgood and Tannenbaum scaled these relationships according to the intensity of the liking/disliking feelings. They proposed a ±3 scale. A +3 was the strongest liking score, while −3 was the strongest disliking score. Thus, a triangle might have the following values:

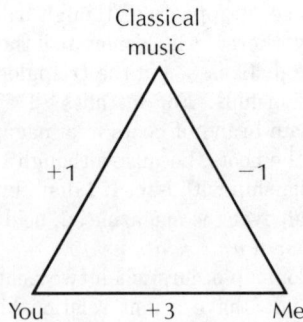

Classical
music

+1   −1

You   +3   Me

Because the liking relationship between you and me (+3) is stronger than either our modest like or dislike for classical music, there would not be much stress produced by this apparently unbalanced triangle. There would be little pressure for either of us to change our minds. But if the situation looked like this:

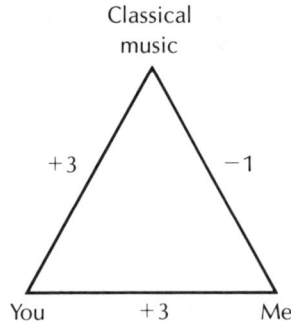

Classical
music

+3   −1

You   +3   Me

there would be a greater amount of pressure for me to change my mind, because my attitude (−1) is the weakest of the set.

More importantly, though, Osgood and Tannenbaum found that under circumstances like the latter, I would not only change my attitude about classical music, but I would also view you a little less favorably for putting me in such a predicament. My attitude toward classical music would change more than would my attitude toward you, because it is the weaker and more vulnerable of the two (−1 versus +3). The stronger the attitude, the more resistant to change it will be.

The point is this. Congruity theory assumes that more than one relationship in a triangle will change in intensity, and those changes will be made toward a "middle ground." Both attitudes will change to become more congruous with each other; hence the name, congruity. The implication of this is that whenever you persuade someone to change his or her mind on a topic to agree more with your feelings, you stand to lose some credibility with that person.

In sum, the modifications proposed by Osgood and Tannenbaum improve balance theory in two ways. First, the relationships can be scaled in intensity so that their relative strength can be denoted. Second, the dynamics of consistency are more accurately described in that a change in one relationship can be accompanied by a change in the other relationship. When people are forced to change their minds about the topic, they reconsider their feelings about the speaker as well. The amount of change in either relationship will be a function of the original intensity of the attitudes. The stronger attitudes will remain more stable, while the weaker ones will shift more.

Applications to HIP

At this point, you might be wondering how balance and congruity fit HIP. On the surface, these theories seem to describe interpersonal relationships more than intrapersonal feelings. But what underlies P−O−X? Isn't the crux of these theories your internal feelings or your attitudes? And to the degree that attitudes influence how you process information, the theories are relevant to HIP.

These theories explain how you need to keep your internal feelings about ideas and people in harmony. They also reveal how your attitudes vary in intensity. Furthermore, they suggest that your stronger feelings will have more impact on your

HIP than will the weaker ones. Suppose I dislike you and you tell me that my father embezzled from a company years ago. What do you predict will be my reaction? I wouldn't believe you. I respect my father's integrity and would have no grounds for believing what you say, especially since I don't like you anyway. You see, my attitudes affect what information I choose to believe and integrate into my prior understanding. Information that fits well with what I know and already believe is easier to adopt than is information that is inconsistent with my stored feelings. Information, whether it be objective or subjective, needs to be reconciled with *both* your cognitive and affective components.

COGNITIVE DISSONANCE

One of the more intriguing and somewhat novel theories of consistency is Festinger's dissonance theory (1957). Compared with the prior two approaches, dissonance theory has generated more excitement and research than any other attitude-change theory.

Most of the excitement and controversy began with a study by Festinger and Carlsmith (1959) in which individual subjects were enlisted to participate in a very boring experimental task of knob-turning and spool-packing for one hour. At the end of the hour, the subject was asked to "assist" the experimenter in greeting the next subject who would perform the same task. The subject's assistance was needed because "the experimenter's regular assistant failed to show up to help with the experiment." The enlisted assistant's job was to meet the next subject and explain how the task was fun and worthwhile. Payment for assisting was either $1 (low reward) or $20 (high reward). The payment was the experimental manipulation— some received low payment, others high payment.

After dutifully fulfilling the assistant role, the subject was interviewed in another room and asked to indicate how enjoyable he or she considered the task (i.e., attitude toward the experiment). The results showed that there was a significant difference between the attitudes of those paid $1 compared with those paid $20. Which group do you think had the more positive attitude?

If you feel that the $20 group should have a more favorable attitude toward the task, you are reasoning from an incentive position. In other words, you feel that people who are rewarded well will feel better about their efforts than those who are not rewarded well. This is a common belief in our society. On the other hand, if you reason that the $1 group would have a more favorable attitude toward the task, you are arguing from the dissonance position.

Justification

The actual results of this study showed that the people who were paid $1 exhibited more favorable attitudes toward the task than did the $20 group. The reason for such a finding rests on the justification process inherent in serving as the assistant. Those in the well-paid condition could justify their lying to the next subject by believing that they were "bought." In other words, given sufficient payment they were willing to lie and still believe that the task was boring. Those in the other condition ($1 payment) could not justify their lying by the rather modest payment for doing so. Given that they couldn't lean on the money as their reason, they were forced to reconsider their original feelings and begin thinking that the task was "really more interesting and worthwhile" than they initially thought.

Postdecisional Dissonance

It is important to recognize that dissonance is not a theory of rewards, but rather a theory of justification. The money paid in the Festinger and Carlsmith study was simply a vehicle to test the incentive versus dissonance position. Anytime you do something difficult, you can experience dissonance. You may even experience postdecisional regret (wishing you hadn't done the regrettable act). This brings us to a key point. Dissonance is a postdecisional state. You may experience some stress before making a decision, but you will not experience dissonance until after you make a decision (Figure 8.4).

Figure 8.4   Dissonance as a postdecisional state.

Festinger suggests that the magnitude of dissonance that a person experiences is a function of a number of things. The intensity of the predecisional conflict makes a difference. For instance, if you are toying with the idea of buying a new car, and after shopping for a month or so, you narrow your choices to, say, a Chevrolet or a Ford, you should experience some dissonance after you choose one over the other. Let's say you chose the Chevrolet. You have resolved your conflict, but now your decision makes you vulnerable to dissonance. How much dissonance you labor under is a function of the attractiveness of the unchosen alternative (Ford). If at the time of your decision you were unable to declare one choice a "clear winner" because of its greater number of advantages over the other, your decision may be made by a mental coin toss. The more equally attractive the two choices, the harder it is to make a decision, and the more dissonance you will experience afterward. By choosing the Chevrolet, the unique characteristics that you considered attractive in the Ford are not available to you. You made your decision; now you have to live with it. How?

Selective Exposure

How do people cope with dissonance? Since dissonance is stressful, it must be resolved in some manner. Festinger (1957) suggests that through selective exposure, people will seek out information that reinforces their decision and avoid information that reminds them of the unchosen alternative. After buying the Chevrolet, you might find yourself reading the newspaper ads from Chevrolet dealers while ignoring the Ford ads. By deliberately reading the ads that support your decision, you are selectively exposing yourself to information consistent with your choice.

While the avoidance of dissonance-arousing information is a basic tenet of this theory, the research testing this avoidance behavior has not been entirely supportive. Brehm and Cohen (1962) found that people did indeed seek dissonance-reducing information, but they did not necessarily avoid counterinformation. Freedman and Sears (1966) also concluded that people do not avoid nonsupportive information. On the other side, Mills (1966) did find that under some conditions people do avoid negative information.

Do these conflicting research findings negate dissonance theory? Absolutely not. Although it is reasonable to expect that people would avoid dissonance-producing information after they made their decisions, it is just as reasonable to assume that the decision process armed them with enough reasons to form a good defense against any arguments questioning their choice. Thus, it may be that after working to make a decision, people test the "quality" of the decision by perusing material on the unchosen alternative just to remind them of their original prudence. I once bought a house after surveying more than ten homes in other tracts. The following Sunday, I found myself going through the newspaper ads on the "other" tracts, noting the "good" things about those homes but also reminding myself of a significant disadvantage of each. I was not avoiding dissonant information; I was simply rehearsing the prudence of my earlier decision.

Over the past 20 years, dissonance theory has provoked hundreds of studies testing its propositions. Since its inception, the original dissonance theory has been modified to account for new findings. These modifications have not, however, shown dissonance theory to be incorrect. As Greenwald and Ronis (1978) recently noted, dissonance theory has changed greatly over the years, but it has never effectively been proven wrong.*

Resolving Inconsistency

Whenever you find yourself in a state of inconsistency, you have a number of options in coping with that stressful situation. Festinger (1957) suggests four alternatives. Let's examine these through a hypothetical situation. Suppose a classmate tells you that your best friend called you a liar at a party last night. Since you were not at the party you didn't witness this happening. Let's further assume that because you like your best friend you are having a hard time dealing with the news. The first thing you can do is to distort the message you just received from your classmate (option 1). You might say that your classmate "really meant to say that my friend said I kid around a lot." By changing the message in a favorable way, you avoid the inconsistency. If that doesn't work, you might derogate the source of the inconsistent information (option 2). You question the credibility of your informant. Your next alternative (option 3) is to leave the field. Try to ignore the message. Pretend you didn't hear it. Don't talk to that person anymore. If none of these options work, then you may be forced to change your attitude about your best friend (option 4). Since this one is the hardest to initiate, because it calls for some internal reorganization of your attitudes, you will probably do all you can before making the necessary change in attitudes.

You should learn from these options that inconsistency does not guarantee that a person will change his or her attitude about the topic. Even the best-laid persuasive messages, using impeccable logic to expose the listener's inconsistent attitudes, will not meet with immediate acquiescence. Most people will resist changing their attitudes in favor of one of the first three options.

Applications to HIP

How does dissonance theory fit into HIP? In what ways can you apply a theory of postdecisional discomfort to gathering, storing, and retrieving information? The

---

*For the reader who finds this controversy interesting and worth pursuing, I would recommend a close reading of Festinger's book, *A Theory of Cognitive Dissonance* (Stanford: Stanford University Press, 1957), before investigating the more current research.

answer lies in selectivity. Dissonance is uncomfortable. People prefer harmony over disharmony. People will, therefore, filter incoming information to test for potential conflicts with what they already know and believe. New information will not be adopted if it sharply conflicts with existing expectations, meanings, and attitudes. Wanting to avoid discomfort, you will selectively attend, perceive, and recall information. Only under circumstances wherein you wish to test the soundness of your cognitive and affective components would you seek dissonance-producing information.

SUMMARY

According to the theories presented in this chapter, "good mental health" assumes that you will work to maintain consistency among your values, attitudes, and beliefs. Whenever your feelings are rocked by an apparent inconsistency, you will find ways to restore your previous state of harmony. Three theories were discussed to explain how you readjust attitudes to restore consistency. Each theory examines a slightly different aspect of consistency restoration, but each underscores the need for it.

Current research in consistency restoration reveals that people have a certain amount of tolerance for inconsistency. Not every case of inconsistency is strong enough to force you to regain consistency. But whenever a person's limits (tolerance) for inconsistency have been exceeded, that person will work to restore consistency, using one of the four methods for resolving inconsistency.

Finally, you should now realize that both the cognitive component (meanings and language) and the affective component (attitudes and self-concepts) serve as the main data bases for filtering incoming and outgoing information. You do not comprehend information nor do you produce information without referring to the cognitive and affective components. Your memory would be sorely lacking and your communication would be highly restricted if you didn't have meanings, language, attitudes, and self-concepts.

SUMMARY PROPOSITIONS

1. Balance theory is based on maintaining harmonious relationships between you and others on common topics.

2. People prefer balanced situations over unbalanced ones.

3. The effect of balance depends on unit relationships and on timing.

4. Congruity theory expands on balance theory by adding the intensity of the attitudes to the P–O–X triangles.

5. When two attitudes are inconsistent with each other, both will change toward a "middle ground."

6. Dissonance theory is a postdecisional approach to attitudes.

7. Dissonance theory demonstrates how people justify their feelings and behavior.

8. People tend to seek postdecisional information that reinforces their decision.

9. When faced with inconsistency, people have four options for resolving it.

10. Your affective and cognitive components serve as filters for incoming and outgoing information.

5 OPERATIONAL COMPONENT

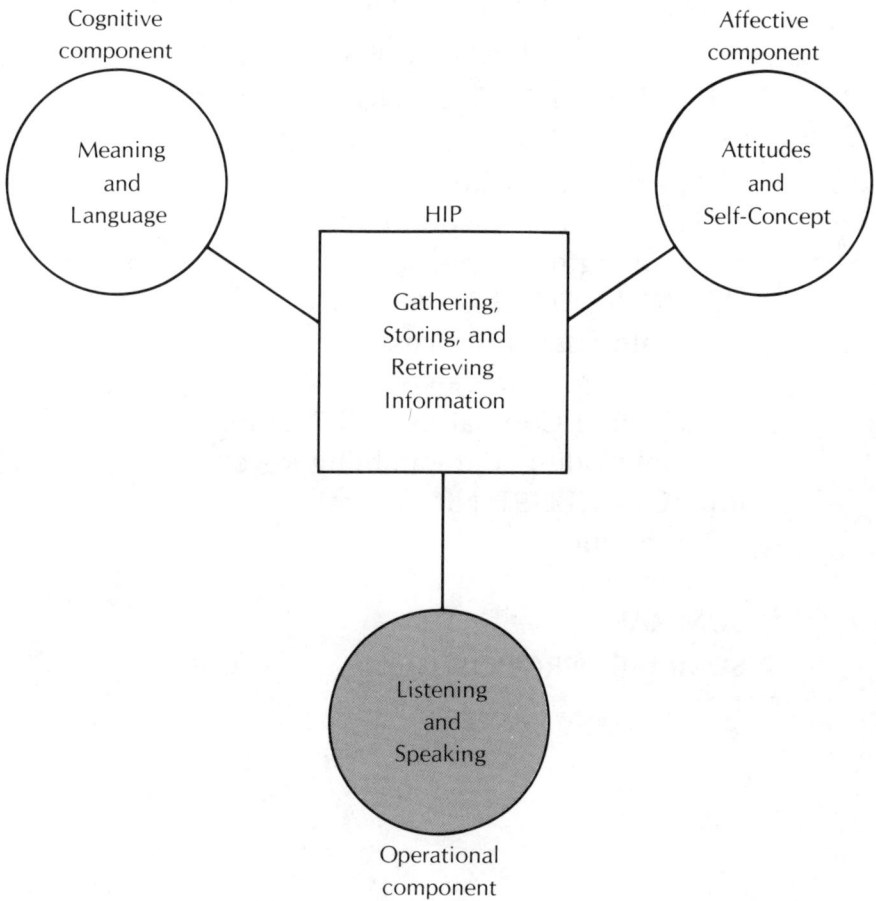

Cognitive
component

Affective
component

Meaning
and
Language

Attitudes
and
Self-Concept

HIP

Gathering,
Storing, and
Retrieving
Information

Listening
and
Speaking

Operational
component

Chapter 9

ENCODING AND DECODING
HEARING VERSUS LISTENING
SELECTIVITY IN LISTENING
REQUIREMENTS FOR LISTENING
    Speech Recognition
    Readiness to Respond
    Meaningful Response
LISTENING COMPREHENSION
    Innate Speech Processor
    Listening Strategies
    Listening Compared with Reading
    Dual Coding and Rambling Recall
IMPROVING LISTENING
    Step One
    Step Two
SUMMARY
SUMMARY PROPOSITIONS

Listening

With this chapter, you begin a study of the operational component of the intrapersonal processes of communication. In oral communication, listening is your main way of taking in information. How effectively you listen can determine what information you have available to store and retrieve. Any breakdowns in listening can cause future shortcomings in recall.

Listening is HIP in action. As you will see shortly, listening is more than hearing. It is a psychological process. Your listening habits are determined by a number of things, not the least of which are your cognitive and affective components. Since listening is such a major part of how you gather information, you need to know more about it.

In this chapter, I will discuss encoding and decoding, the differences between hearing and listening, the selectivity of listening, and the requirements for listening. Then I will consider listening comprehension. The final section will be on improving listening. When you finish reading this chapter, you should have a good understanding of the listening process.

ENCODING AND DECODING

Most cognitive psychologists believe that HIP centers around the process of *coding*. In fact, researchers at the Haskins Laboratories argue that information at different stages of processing requires different codes (Liberman, Mattingly, and Turvey 1972). The code used for saying something (acoustical) is not the same code that is used for storage of information (semantic). This implies, then, that the coding processes used in HIP are not a simple *decode–encode* situation. Coding involves both internal and external decoding and encoding. In other words, when assigning meaning to an utterance, you decode the message, then encode it into your memory for future use. At retrieval, you decode what you have stored in memory and then encode it into a message that others may understand. The process follows a decode–encode–decode–encode pattern (called *DEDE*). Thus, you can see that listening and speaking are bridged by storing and retrieving.

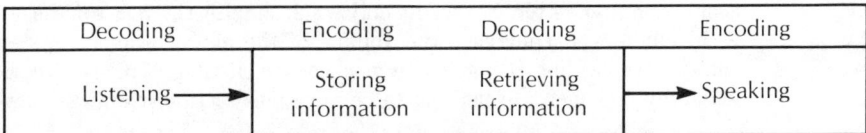

Decoding	Encoding	Decoding	Encoding
Listening⟶	Storing information	Retrieving information	⟶Speaking

Figure 9.1 The DEDE pattern of coding in HIP.

Figure 9.1 illustrates that the communication activities of listening and speaking are intricately linked with the HIP functions of storing and retrieving information. What permits the interfacing of listening with storing (and retrieving with speaking) is the coding process itself. In this sense, then, listening is the process of coding incoming information for storage in memory.

Now let's turn to the listening process and see how this marvelous psychological process allows you to function as a receiver in human communication.

HEARING VERSUS LISTENING

Hearing and listening are not the same. Hearing is the function of the ear. Listening is the work of the mind. When you are hearing you are taking in sounds. When you are listening you are interpreting what you hear. Because the ear cannot resist signals sent to it, whereas the mind can, you tend to listen to less than what is available to you through hearing. The difference between hearing and listening is primarily a matter of selective attention. Out of the array of sound waves pounding on the eardrums, you select those vibrations that you want to listen to. You choose what you want to make sense of. In essence, then, listening is hearing with selective attention.

So far, I have been talking about listening in general. It is time to define listening as it applies to communication. When you listen to verbal messages, you must structure the sounds that strike the eardrums so that you perceive them as words, phrases, and sentences. Listening, then, is the process of taking what you hear and organizing it into verbal units to which you can apply meaning. You and I use our language so much that it is easy to forget that we structure speech sounds when we listen. I, too, overlooked the necessity for perceiving speech as separate units of language until I read Neisser's comments about foreign languages (Neisser 1976). He notes that it is much easier to listen to your own language compared with a foreign language. He observes that "all of us have schematic anticipations for the structured sounds of our own language; that is why we hear them as distinct and separate words while the talk of foreigners often appears to be an almost continuous stream" (p. 27). His point is well taken. Unless you know how to perceive the language spoken, it is impossible to understand it. Listening, then, is dependent on the listener being able to structure the speech sounds into recognizable language units.

SELECTIVITY IN LISTENING

Listening is a selective activity. It is a process of filtering. Your filters come from your cognitive and affective components. Even when you try to suppress any psychological biases that you may have, you still listen selectively. I became painfully aware of this when I first started wearing a hearing aid for a mild to moderate hearing loss. The first thing I noticed about my artificially improved hearing was that I was able to hear *everything* better. My aid not only would amplify the voices of those I was talking with, but it would increase the volume of the air-conditioning system, the birds outside, the rattling change in my pocket, the rustling of paper. Needless to say, I found my new world of hearing to be very noisy. (I don't know how you stand it.)

Eventually, I learned to screen out the background noises and concentrate on the messages I wanted to listen to. By necessity, then, listening has to be selective.

Another example of selective listening comes from a study I cited in Chapter 3. You might remember the "cocktail party problem." That was Cherry's term for how people are able to choose from a number of competing conversations those messages relevant to their interests. In his laboratory study of this phenomenon, Cherry (1953) had people listen to two different messages being presented simultaneously by headphones in different ears. As instructed by Cherry, the subjects could easily attend to one message while rejecting the other message in the other ear. Furthermore, when asked to repeat one of the messages aloud while both messages were being presented (shadowing), Cherry found that people had no difficulty doing so. Their speech, however, turned out to be fairly monotonous, with very little stress on important words. The important thing about this study, however, is the relative ease with which people were able to reject the other message and focus on the relevant message. When the messages were similar in content and form, however, the task became much more difficult. The more dissimilar the messages, the easier it is to reject the unwanted one. It is easier to listen to someone talk with a noisy fan going than it is with someone else also talking. Apparently, the key to listening is not so much the focusing of attention on the desired message as it is the successful rejection of similar and distracting messages. This is an important point, since it is often necessary to remove distractions before you can "home in" on one signal. Good listening calls for the rejection of unwanted distractions.

REQUIREMENTS FOR LISTENING

Let's now look more specifically at the workings of listening. Rather than going into detail about auditory processing or neurological structures and the anatomy of the ear, I want to pose some minimal conditions necessary for listening, particularly accurate listening. Under the assumption that the listener has properly functioning ears and that the speech signal is sufficiently strong to be heard, three requirements must be met for the processing of speech.

Speech Recognition

The first requirement is speech recognition. As a listener you must be able to distinguish when a sound is a speech sound and when it is not. This may seem like a trivial task to you, but to the newborn infant exposed to a noisy world, this is a crucial step in understanding speech. Not all sounds are speech signals intended for symbolic consumption; some sounds are simply noise. Not only do you have to know the difference between noise and speech, you must be able to distinguish different sounds in speech. In other words, you must be able to survey the speech signal itself and decide what word(s) the sounds comprise.

Although the average rate of natural speech is approximately 150 words per minute, some interesting research on compressed speech (speeding up the message three to four times its natural rate) shows that people are able to discriminate speech sounds presented at 400 to 500 words per minute (Orr 1968). What this finding demonstrates is that you are equipped to deal with speech even at fast rates. The initial stage of listening, then, is simply recognizing the speech signal.

Readiness to Respond

The second requirement for listening is that you must be ready to respond to the message. This implies several things. First, you must not be too tired to attend to the message. You have to devote a certain amount of energy to listening, and if you don't have it, you can't listen very well. Next, you have to have psychological readiness. You can't be heavily involved in one thing and try to listen to another. In fact, a good definition of an interruption is anything that demands your attention when you want to continue to devote it to something else. If you are not busy, you cannot be interrupted. Being alert and in the right frame of mind are prerequisites for being ready to listen.

Being ready to respond to the speech signal has been documented as a vital part of listening by a number of researchers who study how people listen to spoken messages. Controlled laboratory studies show that when people give their attention to the spoken message, they are able to follow even fast-moving messages. Cole and Jakimik (1978) found that in listening for speech, ". . . word recognition is fast. The listener is probably not more than one or possibly two words behind the speaker" (p. 113). So, you are equipped to follow speech, if you will only give it your attention.

Meaningful Response

The final requirement is your ability to respond meaningfully. You must somehow know what people are talking about. You must understand the words (code) and have meanings to assign to the words. Recent research tells us that listeners look for a point of view or a theme (Black, Turner, and Bower 1979) through which they can make sense out of the message. They are able to respond meaningfully when they apply an underlying point of view to the message.

You see, you need to be able to do more than recognize words; you have to assign meaning. Very young children have trouble following adult conversations at the dinner table, not because thy don't hear what is said or recognize some of the words, but because they do not have sufficient meanings for the words they hear. To understand, you must be able to recognize the words and choose appropriate meanings that fit the theme of the message. Furthermore, the meanings must be in you, because they are not in the words. At best, the words are signals for meanings that you must already have. If you have meaning for a message, you can understand it. If you don't, you can't.

Therefore, listening requires that you (1) recognize speech, (2) be prepared to respond, and (3) be able to respond meaningfully. By doing these three things, you will be able to analyze any set of speech sounds by structuring them into words, phrases, and sentences that you can interpret. Until you organize the sounds into language units, you are simply hearing, not listening. Listening is more than simply sensing sounds. You must do something with those sounds in order to listen.

LISTENING COMPREHENSION

With the prerequisites for listening out of the way, I can turn to describing how you perceive speech and comprehend what is said through listening. This is a very popular area of research—one that is producing some new ideas about listening. The possibility of an inborn speech processor is one of those exciting ideas.

Innate Speech Processor

Research in speech perception investigates a very early age. Working with infants under six months old, Eimas (1974) offers data that show that, even at a very young age, humans are especially able to discriminate speech sounds from other sounds. In fact, Eimas' research indicates that infants as young as one month old can differentiate among speech sounds, as well as recognize speech sounds apart from other noises. This means that babies can meet the first requirement for listening (speech recognition) without much exposure to the external world.

These kinds of findings have led other researchers (Liberman 1972) to speculate that humans may have an innate processor specially designed for speech perception. In other words, you may have arrived in this world with an inborn ability to recognize speech and discriminate some of its sounds. Liberman thinks that this ability is tied into your advanced speech-making apparatus. Humans are equipped for producing speech sounds, and this may make you and me immediately ready to deal with speech when we are born. This had led many researchers to reconsider the once-popular notion that language is innate at birth. If researchers like Eimas are correct, you may be "wired" for speech perception, from which language learning develops. At this time, it is safest to conclude that you have an innate capability for processing speech, but that you are not born with a knowledge of language.

Listening Strategies

Even though you may be uniquely prepared for listening because of your speech processor, listening itself is not automatic. It is not like a continuously running fan that circulates the air in your room. Listening is a deliberate act. It involves strategies. You use listening strategies to determine what someone is saying to you. Your listening strategies help you answer the question, "What does the speaker mean?"

In 1974, Aronson surveyed a number of studies of listening comprehension. From her review of the literature, Aronson generated a number of hypotheses about strategies for listening. Three of those propositions will be mentioned here. First, Aronson observed that people use the pauses found in a speaker's natural speaking pattern to process what is being said. They take the very brief time afforded by pauses to decipher the message. This does not mean that listeners wait for pauses before processing the message. They process the message as it is being said, but they use the pauses to think about the message rather than waiting for the next point. If there are not enough pauses or if the pauses are not sufficient in length, listening is made more difficult. Likewise, too many pauses or pauses of too long a duration bog down the speech perception process.

Second, Aronson found that the relative level of redundancy and predictability of our language allows time to process the content of the sentences. In other words, when two people interact with each other, they do not have to search for the meaning of each word. They need to listen for the content words, which carry the main ideas, while monitoring the other words, which serve primarily a grammatical function. This means that people don't need to understand each word thoroughly to comprehend the sentence. In fact, research shows that it is possible to eliminate just about every other word from a message without seriously harming the listener's understanding of the message. When faced with such mutilated messages, listeners fill in what they think is missing and thus comprehend the message (Taylor 1956). If our language were not as predictable as it is, people could not do this.

Finally, Aronson notes that listening probably involves a rapid predict–then–confirm strategy. Given the amount of time provided in normal conversation by pauses and redundancy, you are apparently able to predict what is coming up in a sentence and then wait to see if it occurs. Most of the time, your predictions are correct. You may not hit the exact words, but you should be able to identify and project the general ideas. When you fail to predict correctly, it is typically due to your own ignorance about the topic. The more you know about what the speaker is talking about, the easier it will be for you to predict. You might also be unsuccessful in predicting the outcome of a sentence because of humor. If someone is trying to be funny and you don't realize it, you might be caught off guard by the punch line. Effective humor is based upon upsetting the normal predict–then–confirm strategy of listening. What makes you laugh at a joke is the surprise you encounter at the end of it. The predict–then–confirm strategy of listening indicates that listening is a guessing game. As long as things remain predictable, you can guess correctly, and thus listen effectively.

A discussion of listening strategies would be incomplete if I didn't acknowledge the fact that when you listen you attend to more than the words. You listen to the tone of voice (paralanguage), and you attend to the accompanying gestures (kinesics). In essence, listening in a face-to-face conversation means that you take account of all the relevant messages. Each message helps you determine what the speaker means.

Listening Compared with Reading

A good way to learn more about listening comprehension is to compare it with reading comprehension. The key question here is whether the way you learn information affects the amount of recall you have for it. In other words, do you recall differently information that you heard compared with information that you read? Or is recall the same regardless of how you acquired it?

Research that compares listening comprehension with reading comprehension reveals that the method of intake does make a difference. Walker (1975– 76) found that people who read a story, then recalled it, did so with greater precision than people who listened to the story but didn't read it. Walker found that reading comprehension was more accurate than listening comprehension. In this sense, precision and accuracy refer to the closeness of the recalled versions to the actual wording of the original version. This means that when recall needs to be more consistent with the original wording, then reading the material would be better than listening to it. In another study Horowitz and Berkowitz (1967) found that listeners (compared with readers) of material produced a larger corpus of information (more total recall in terms of length), more ideas, fewer omissions of important units, more distortions, and more repetitions of information. In other words, when you recall information that you heard, you tend to produce a story that is longer, wordier, more comprehensive in coverage, but flawed with incorrect interpretations of some of the original information.

Combining the results of the above studies, you can conclude that reading information helps you have a more precise recollection of the original wording. However, recalling information that you heard leads to longer stories that are more complete in coverage but likely to have errors in them. There are advantages to both. If you need accuracy, read it. If you need breadth of coverage, listen to it. By both listening to it and reading it, you can have a more accurate image of the original wording. That is why taking notes in class is so important. By listening to the lecture and having a set of notes to refer to, you increase your chances of recalling the information at test time. And like everything else in HIP, the more actively involved you become with information, the more you will remember the information later.

Dual Coding and Rambling Recall

Why is listening comprehension different from reading comprehension? Basically the answer comes down to two issues: dual coding and rambling recall. *Dual coding* refers to your storing information in two different ways. Whenever you see and hear something, you store it in auditory memory and in visual memory. Thus, it is coded twice—once as a visual image, and again as a verbal message. Reading is often accomplished through dual coding, which is why it is more accurate. Many people see the words on the page and then say them through "silent speech." They silently utter the message as they are reading it, thus dual coding the message. Anything that is stored and coded twice has a good chance of being recalled verbatim (provided, of course, that there has been sufficient rehearsal of the message). When listening, people may not take advantage of dual coding. They just hear the words; they do not spell them out in their minds. Reading comprehension, then, should be more verbatim than listening comprehension.

The second reason for the recall differences in listening versus reading is in what I call *rambling recall*. Rambling recall is telling a story in such a way that you correct yourself and add details as you go along. Under these conditions, the story is not too well organized, but it covers the territory. This kind of recall occurs especially when you are retelling a story aloud rather than writing it. I'm sure that you have experienced the problem of not being able to tell the same story twice. Since oral stories are created "on the spot," they are hard to duplicate. The very nature of speech permits more rambling. And this gives you an opportunity to "improve" on a story every time you tell it.

Oral recall of information that was originally heard and not read is subject to wide diversity. Although you can create a story that is generally consistent with the original version, it will not be an exact duplication of it. Unless you have memorized information word-for-word, your oral recall will be a paraphrase of your memory. I'll talk more about this in the next chapter.

In summary, listening comprehension is possible because you are especially equipped to deal with the speech signal. When you listen, you use the pauses and the redundancy in the message to predict–then–confirm what is coming up in the message. Listening comprehension results in different recall than does reading comprehension. You will be more accurate recalling information you read, but you will be more thorough when recalling information that you heard. Whenever possible, it is best to see *and* hear information.

IMPROVING LISTENING

From time to time I am asked, "What can I do to improve my listening skills?" There are many tricks that you can use to improve listening. You can have a tape recorder handy. You can nod frequently at the speaker so he or she will talk directly to you. You can compare notes with other listeners later on. You can mentally push aside your prejudices so that they do not inhibit your listening. All these bits of advice are useful, but in reality, good listening comes down to two steps.

Step One

More than anything else, you need to isolate the message you want to listen to. Somehow that message must stand out from the array of messages coming at you at once. It is easier to recall information that you have successfully isolated than it is to recall messages that were blended into the background of all the other messages. This is called the Von Restorff effect. Simply stated, items that you isolate as unique are easier to recall than items that are common to previous items. Research supporting this effect is plentiful (Newman and Saltz 1958; Green 1958). So look for the unique features of any bit of information you wish to remember.

Another way of isolating the input is to avoid distractions from unwanted messages. Information comes at you in a competitive fashion. You must decide what to listen to. It is similar to the I/N ratio I talked about in Chapter 3. By elevating the desired input to information (in the I/N ratio) while reducing the other inputs to noise, you can devote the proper amount of energy to the message you want to remember. Research shows that when you cannot screen out distractions and lower them to noise, your recall will suffer (Bryant and Comisky 1978).

So, the first thing you can do to improve your listening is to isolate the input by looking for unique features and by removing distracting messages that compete for your attention. The more actively involved you can become in a clearly focused line of attention, the more you will recall what you learned.

Step Two

The second thing you can do to improve your listening comprehension is to look for structure and ideas, not for words. Sometimes people get so anxious about remembering "all this information" that they try to memorize the exact wording. But if the message is long, memorization is almost impossible without an additional device for recording the message for study later.

In everyday communication, you do not need to memorize what people say. You need to get the gist of what they say. Thus, you should pay attention to the reasoning and to the ideas being presented rather than trying to recall the exact words. Hulse, Deese, and Egeth (1975 p. 417) argue quite correctly that when it comes to listening to meaningful material like everyday conversations, you retain the meaning of the conversation more than the words. Likewise, Garner (1974 p.186) believes that it is natural for you to find structure in what you encounter. In fact, he suggests that most of the world that you attend to is pretty well structured, so you don't have to provide much structure yourself.

Day-to-day listening, then, is made simpler if you isolate the desired message and look for the main points being made. If you have to listen more analytically, you will need additional assistance provided by note-taking or other devices for recording the conversation. For those of you interested in listening in the classroom, check the Appendix of this book. There you will find a brief set of recommendations on taking notes and studying for exams.

SUMMARY

Listening is, by design, selective. It assumes that you can recognize speech, are ready to respond, and can respond meaningfully. Those signals that seem irrelevant, unrecognizable, or potentially meaningless will not demand much of your listening time.

Speaking of time, listening takes time. You use the speaker's pauses and the inherent redundancy in our language to decide what the speaker means. Listening is best characterized as a rapid predict–then–confirm activity. You listen long enough to make a decision. You don't have to have the complete message before you to begin your guessing game.

You also learned in this chapter that listening comprehension differs from reading comprehension. Since you don't actually see what is being said (you hear it), you don't use dual coding. This makes your recall less verbatim and often more "creative" as you tell others what you originally heard.

Finally, you observed that improving listening depends on your success at isolating the input and looking for ideas rather than simply words.

SUMMARY PROPOSITIONS

1. Listening and speaking are processes of decoding and encoding.
2. Decoding and encoding follow a DEDE pattern (decoding–encoding–decoding–encoding).
3. Listening is selective hearing.
4. Listening is the process of taking what you hear and organizing it into verbal units that you can apply meaning to.
5. There are three requirements for listening:
   a. speech recognition.
   b. readiness to respond.
   c. ability to respond meaningfully.
6. You may be born with an innate processor for speech signals.
7. Listening comprehension follows a predict–then–confirm strategy.
8. Listening comprehension tends to be different from reading comprehension.
9. To improve listening, you should find ways to isolate the desired input and to look for structure.

Chapter 10

SPONTANEOUS SPEECH
  Interface of Language, Speech, and Meaning
  Planning and Monitoring
  Summary
NATURAL SPEECH OUTPUT
  Length of Utterances
  Speech Errors
  Speaking Rate
  Vocabulary
  Nonfluencies
  Pausing
  Summary
PARAPHRASING
  Creating Sentences
SCHEMATA
  Using Schemata
  Schemata and Themes
  Schemata and Conversation
  Making Inferences
  Logical and Pragmatic Implications
SUMMARY
SUMMARY PROPOSITIONS

Speaking

In a typical day you will spend more time speaking and listening than you will writing and reading. Research shows that oral communication clearly dominates your total communication time. Speaking is the means by which you orally encode your ideas. Speaking allows you to express yourself and elicit responses from other people. The ability to speak is very important to you, but unless you face chronic speech fright, you probably don't worry much about your speaking skills.

Most of your speaking activity takes place in casual conversations. You and your friends talk about a number of topics with relative ease. Sometimes you may even argue. But most of you are sufficiently competent in speaking to be able to participate in everyday conversations. But have you ever wondered how you can be reasonably fluent in casual conversations without planning everything you say? In casual conversations, your speech is spontaneous; it is not formal. If you don't plan your spontaneous speech, why does it seem to come out all right most of the time? The answer to this question is what this chapter is all about.

In this chapter I will examine how spontaneous speech occurs. Then I will look at natural speech output to discover what it is typically like. The final sections will cover paraphrasing and schemata—two cognitive skills that make spontaneous speaking possible.

SPONTANEOUS SPEECH

For the most part, most of your daily interactions are impromptu. Rarely do you find youself in formal public speaking situations (unless it is part of your work). Yet, people value thoughtful speech and appreciate someone who is able to converse comfortably with others. A good conversationalist is one who participates well in spontaneous speech. But what is spontaneous speech and how does it work?

Spontaneous speech is the act of creating your words and sentences at the time you are speaking. It is choosing your words just before you actually say them. Setting aside various speech handicaps, everyone speaks spontaneously. Your spontaneous speech results in a set of sentences that express your meanings. Interestingly enough, most sentences that you produce in a day are unique, except in obvious ceremonial speech.

Interface of Language, Speech, and Meaning

How does your spontaneous speech result in a number of unique sentences? What are the conditions necessary for spontaneous speech to occur? Spontaneous speech

99

occurs when you engage your understanding of the language, a set of speech rules, and a theme or idea to be communicated to someone. By successfully interfacing language, speech, and meaning, you accomplish correctness, relevance, and meaningfulness. Another way of saying this is that you use the rules of language to form grammatically correct sentences; you apply your understanding of social speaking rules to say something that is relevant to the conversation; and finally, you choose words that represent what you have stored in memory. When these three interface with one another, you can create messages as you are speaking. Exactly how you are able to do this is still being researched, but that you and I are able to do so is rarely questioned.

Planning and Monitoring

One explanation for spontaneous speech comes from Lindsley (1975), who argues that people do not plan sentences in their entirety; rather, people plan phrases. Since sentences often involve more than one thought, you plan your speech by thought units. Sentences are, in this case, grammatical conveniences for saying what is on your mind. If a sentence has two thoughts in it, you spontaneously plan each thought separately as you are talking. When you are finished, you have a sentence; but when you started, you had phrases. Lindsley would argue, then, that people speak in phrases that can be organized into sentences. Since it is easier to plan phrases than it is to plan complete sentences, spontaneous speech is accomplished through phrase planning.

Another aspect of spontaneous speech is monitoring. As you speak spontaneously, you listen to yourself. By listening to what you are saying you can correct your mistakes during the sentence, as you typically do. If you have difficulty finding the right word or expression, it is usually in the middle of a sentence. As you monitor your own speech, you are probably not more than a word or two "behind your mouth." Thus, you can stop to make your corrections before finishing the sentence.

The concept of monitoring your own speech through self-feedback has generated interest among researchers dealing with spontaneous speech. Yates (1963) found that if he artificially delayed a speaker's self-feedback, the speaker would have trouble continuing a smooth speech pattern. Imagine what it would be like to be talking, but not hearing yourself until several seconds later. Nathan (1969) points out that one reason that deaf people do not develop perfectly smooth speech patterns is that they cannot hear their own speech: "Their speech is slow and often nasal . . . the intensity of the sounds they produce varies greatly, and they are liable to make loud noises with breathing, gasping, or sighing" (p. 305). As you can see, spontaneous speech depends not only on the voice mechanisms but on the feedback provided by the ears as well. Most hearing people would probably become reticent if they couldn't monitor their own speech. How about you?

Summary

Spontaneous speech is the act of making up your sentences as you go along. In such impromptu speaking you plan what you are going to say by phrases rather than complete sentences. To produce spontaneous speech you retrieve an idea from semantic memory, and you combine your knowledge of the language and the appropriate speech rules to compose an utterance that expresses your meaning. As you are talking you monitor your own speech to check for errors. If you make an error, you correct it as soon as you detect it, often in the middle of a sentence.

Now that you have an understanding of spontaneous speech, let's look at what spontaneous speaking produces, that is, at actual output.

NATURAL SPEECH OUTPUT

There are several ways to describe natural speech ouput. I will consider the following: length of utterances, speech errors, speaking rate, vocabulary, nonfluencies, and pausing behaviors.

Length of Utterances

James Deese (1978) has provided an excellent descriptive report on the qualities of everyday speech. Among other things, he found that in speech, sentences are very short. An analysis of tape-recorded conversations revealed that 20 percent of the spoken sentences lasted for one second or less. Of the more than 20,000 utterances tabulated, more than 90 percent lasted less than ten seconds. This means that most of your interactions or turns at speaking are quite brief.

Speech Errors

Deese also found that people don't make as many major errors in speaking as they might think. Truly incorrect sentences were rare. Most of the time, speakers were able to correct themselves before finishing the sentence. "Fouled up" sentences accounted for less than 2 percent of all the sentences spoken. As Deese concluded, "deviant sentences result from a failure of monitoring" (p. 316). This statement reinforces the importance of self-feedback mentioned earlier.

Speaking Rate

Not only are most of your utterances short, they are usually spoken at a rate that is easy to follow. On the average, you and I speak at a rate of 150 words per minute. Sometimes we may speak more slowly or more quickly, depending on our emotional state and the immediate situation. For instance, a lecture may be given at 100 words per minute, while a radio newscaster may speak at 175 words per minute. We also experience differences in speaking rate as a function of personality differences. Some people simply speak faster than others. Giles and Powesland (1975) report that people experiencing emotional disturbances speak at a very fast rate and have more nonfluencies than is normal. Thus if you don't want your speech to reflect a "hyper" personality, you may want to slow down your rate, particularly if it is above, say, 200 words per minute.

Varying your speech rate is also desirable in order to gain a favorable response from your receivers. Giles and St. Clair (1979) found that speakers who were willing to adjust their speech rate to accommodate the listeners were seen as more likable, and their messages were judged as more effective. Usually, listeners can take advantage of the redundancy in language to allow them time to follow your meaning without difficulty. But for complex information, it is a good idea to slow down a bit.

Vocabulary

Spontaneous speech seems to have a limited vocabulary. All speakers know more words than they use. The vocabulary of spontaneous speech is smaller than your reading vocabulary, or even your writing vocabulary. Your speaking style is different from your writing style. When speaking you use fewer different words, shorter words, and more action words. One reason for simplifying your speaking style and limiting your vocabulary may be that you don't want to make mistakes in public. In fact, most people have at least one word that they passionately avoid whenever possible. For me, it is the word "abominable." I always pronounce that word "abdomen-able," so I avoid it. I'm sure that you have your "avoid–at–all–cost" words as well. And if you are like me, you know that your self-concept is most vulnerable when you are speaking. People are more willing to struggle with a word they cannot pronounce or don't understand when they are reading in private than when they are speaking. After all, who is going to know if you foul up a word while you're reading?

Nonfluencies

What about norms for good speaking? Is natural speech smooth and free from nonfluencies? Is it to your advantage to be free from speaking errors such as nonfluencies? The answer is "No." Miller and Hewgill (1964) discovered after manipulating speaker nonfluency in a number of ways that the most fluent speaker (without any errors) was not awarded the highest source credibility by the listeners. Audiences prefer speakers who are not so smooth that people begin to distrust them. Rather, the highest credibility ratings went to the speaker who had an occasional nonfluency (such as an "ah," or a repetition). Good conversational style, then, does not need perfect articulation, pitch, or rhythm. In fact, too much of these qualities may call undesirable attention to the speaker rather than to the message.

This suggests that a fast-talking, error-free, flowery speaker may impress an insecure person, but the average person should not be impressed. Natural speech comes from natural people, not from polished public speakers. People have a tendency to overestimate the value of a "good public speaker," and in the process, believe that the merits of effective public speaking lie in delivery. Such is not the case. The effectiveness of any speaker is a combination of many things, of which delivery plays only one part.

Pausing

In spontaneous speech, pausing is common and natural. Some people believe that pausing indicates an uncertainty, or even a weakness, on the speaker's part. Such attitudes are inappropriate. Natural pauses help both the speaker and the listener. The speaker uses them to collect thoughts. The listener uses them for additional processing of the message.

Certainly, long pauses in the middle of thoughts can indicate some cognitive uncertainty. If these elongated pauses occur too frequently, people will become impatient with the speaker. Most people, however, do not have unusually long pausing patterns.

If you listen closely, you will discover that pauses tend to occur between clauses (such as at the ends of phrases and sentences). They also occur within clauses, usually as an "ah" or "uh" sound. Pauses that occur between clauses are grammatical pauses, designed to punctuate speech. Those that occur within clauses are cognitive pauses, designed to let the speaker think. With either kind of pause, the speaker is able to plan the next phrase or idea. Pauses, then, serve planning purposes. And since you plan your speech as you speak, you need pauses to give you time for planning.

Summary

Let's review. Spontaneous speech produces natural speech output that is fairly short, simple in vocabulary, relatively free from major errors, but not devoid of an occasional nonfluency. This kind of message uses both grammatical and cognitive pauses. Natural speech behavior is not a continuous, uninterrupted string of sentences such as occur in a book. Rather, conversations are tattered with interruptions, pauses, and restarts. A typical tape-recorded interaction would look something like this:

Sally: Ted, you sure have lots of stamps in your collection. Do you . . .
Ted: Thank you.
Sally: Do you spend a lot of time with it?
Ted: Oh, yes. In fact, Last week . . . no, it was Monday, not last week . . . anyway . . . I made a great trade with a dealer in Dallas. . . . By the way, did you go to the big game in Dallas last fall?
Sally: I sure did . . . what a mess . . . couldn't get a room . . . we had to sleep in the car.
Ted: That's too bad.

This brief example illustrates that conversations are not necessarily smooth. Topic changes occur. Speakers interrupt each other. People make errors occasionally. But speakers like Sally and Ted have no problem understanding each other. Spontaneous speech produces natural speech behavior that is not perfect, but very adequate for everyday communication.

Now that you understand spontaneous speech and the way it is planned as you are speaking, you need to consider what information processing strategies you use to produce natural, spontaneous speech. In other words, you need to be able to apply HIP to producing oral sentences.

PARAPHRASING

The act of speaking, like the act of recall, is a spontaneous reconstructive process. As you converse with someone else, you create ideas through your speech. You recall ideas from memory and reconstruct them for expression. In order to take individual ideas from memory and share them with someone else, you need to paraphrase them into speech messages. As Liberman, Mattingly, and Turvey (1972) argue, "except in special cases . . . recall is always a paraphrase" (p. 307). They mean that you do not simply duplicate what you have stored in memory to produce recall; in spontaneous speech you paraphrase your meanings using the rules mentioned earlier.

Paraphrasing can be seen in human interactions. As two people converse, they create information between them. As Sally and Ted demonstrated, human interaction is spontaneous. Each contribution to a conversation is a paraphrase of what the speaker is thinking. If we are talking together, my speech can trigger your memory and you can then spontaneously paraphrase your thoughts on the point. By definition, a conversation is a sequence of paraphrased ideas that is brought about by interaction. Thus, paraphrased recall is observable in human communication.

Creating Sentences

Paraphrased ideas come in the form of sentences. But how do you create your sentences as you are paraphrasing? What is the underlying pattern of organization in speaking? First, you must realize that people do not speak in words. They speak in phrases and sentences. In other words, you do not plan each word when you speak; you plan and develop your thoughts. Since the sentence is a convenient way to discuss thoughts, let's see how the sentence is organized to express what you mean.

Whenever you are in the process of constructing a sentence, you operate from the assumption that meanings can be best expressed if they are centered around the verb. Take, for example, this sentence: "Dr. Williams teaches class in Room 207." This sentence is organized around the notion of what Dr. Williams does. He teaches. What? Class. Where? In Room 207. This sentence can be pictorially represented as:

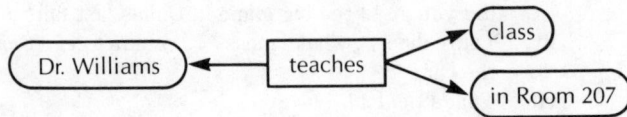

Dr. Williams ← teaches → class / in Room 207

As you can see, the subject and the object are centered around the verb. Organized this way, you can easily construct a sentence that links together three ideas.

Let's try another sentence: "The children in the playground are chasing each other." This one would be diagrammed as:

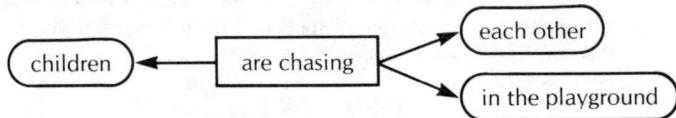

children ← are chasing → each other / in the playground

As before, you can tell what is happening, where it is happening, and to whom it is happening.

One reason for viewing sentences in this way is that recall is more efficient when it is centered around the key linking idea—the verb. As Frank Smith (1975) argues, this is the most efficient way to view sentence processing. By using this strategy for constructing sentences, you can paraphrase ideas from memory in a systematic way.

You need to be careful, at this point, not to assume that all recall must be paraphrased. Some things must be recalled exactly as you have them memorized, for instance, the Pledge of Allegiance, or the lyrics of a song, or the combination to your lock. But when dealing with everyday communication, you don't use this kind of rote memory. For most conversations, you paraphrase, using the verb as the center of your sentences.

Taking this analysis of producing speech a step further, you must ask the question, "How do you conceive of the ideas that are to be represented by *many* sentences?" For instance, how can I, as the author of this text, put together the paragraphs and chapters that you are reading? What are some of the larger strategies that go into larger ideas? The answer lies in schemata.

SCHEMATA

You have many ideas stored in your memory. Some of them are meanings for words that you use frequently. Other ideas are fully developed conceptions that represent all that you know about a given topic. These are called *schemata*. They are your understandings of various concepts. They represent everything you know about a topic. For instance, "washing clothes" is a schema. (Note that *schema* is the singular form of *schemata*.) When you think of washing clothes, you not only know what it is in terms of the formal, functional, and affective aspects of its meaning, you also know many things about it. Likewise, other concepts have schemata. Your idea of "cars," "college education," or "making a living" has a large network of information that makes up your total understanding of that concept. Schemata are your packages of knowledge. Every time you learn something new about a concept, you add it to your schema about that concept.

Using Schemata

Whenever you respond to someone's message about a topic, you incorporate that information into your pre-existing schema (Housel 1981). When you prepare to speak, you call up as much of the schema as you can recall at one time. You refer to your mental schemata when you communicate. In many ways, you use your schemata to construct stories about the topic under discussion. By "stories" I mean explanations and descriptions of all you can remember about something according to how you have it bundled in memory. You use schemata to organize the theme of your talk.

Schemata and Themes

The notion of schemata was first introduced by Bartlett (1932). He conducted a number of experiments in which people were given a story and then asked to retell the story at a later time. As you would expect, most people weren't very good at recalling all the details of the original story. They distorted many facts and added things that weren't present in the original version. But the thing that Bartlett noticed most was that people tended to build stories that made sense. They concocted narratives that fit what they could remember from the original version and filled in gaps with information they knew beforehand. In other words, the people developed themes. And these themes came from their prior knowledge of the topics in the stories. Bruner (1973) describes this as "going beyond the information given." Whenever people talk about something, they elaborate on it, leaning heavily on their mental schema underlying their understanding of the topic.

That people use schemata to assist recall is evidenced in the work of Loftus and Palmer (1974). They showed a group of students a filmed automobile accident. Later they questioned them about some of the details of the accident. In most cases, they found that the students were willing to testify to details about the scene that were not originally present, but were thought to be. For instance, when asked if the headlamp was broken on one of the cars, most of the student witnesses were confident that it was broken. In actuality, the headlamp was still intact after the wreck. Why were they so confident that there was a broken headlamp? The answer lies in the schema of "automobile accidents." To the students, it seemed very plausible that a headlamp would be broken under these circumstances. In their efforts to reconstruct what they saw, they made their recall fit their schemata. This is something we all do.

Schemata and Conversation

You learn to develop a theme from your schemata through communication. As you share information with someone else, you tend to make a "story" based on a running theme or schema. Your schema is the point you are trying to make. One of the things that distinguishes adult speaking behavior from young children's speaking behavior is the presence or absence of a unifying theme. Children often give you bits of information that are not tied together well, or connected with "and then . . . and then . . . and then." Having information presented to you in loosely connected bits means that you have to provide the order to make sense of the story. Fortunately, most adults provide enough of a theme to enable their listeners to understand the messages.

Before going on, I want to emphasize that schemata operate throughout your HIP. You use schemata not only for recalling information, but for comprehending information and for storing it. According to Rumelhart and Ortony (1977), schemata are the main organizing forces for HIP. You comprehend, store, and retrieve information to correspond with all you know about the topic at hand (your schema).

Making Inferences

Without realizing it, people often use schemata to make inferences when they are reconstructing their knowledge for communication. I have already alluded to the fact that recall reconstruction produces inferences that add material not originally present. Paraphrasing and schemata also contribute to your inferential habits. This is best illustrated by the work of Bransford and Franks (1971), who presented people with a series of sentences all related to a single schema. Afterward, they tested for recall. An example of the sentences they used is as follows:

1. The ants were in the kitchen.
2. The jelly was on the table.
3. The jelly was sweet.
4. The ants ate the jelly.

At the time of recall, the subjects were given three different kinds of sentences to identify as to whether they were in the original set. Some of the sentences were exactly as the ones presented earlier, and others were sentences not given before. Some of the new sentences were integrations of two or more of the original sentences. For instance, with the four sentences in the example above, an integrated sentence would be "The ants ate the sweet jelly, which was on the table in the kitchen." When Bransford and Franks asked the subjects if the integrated sentence was part of the original set of sentences, a strikingly large number of people said yes. The researchers interpret this phenomenon as indicating that people take bits of information and integrate them into one whole idea. This whole idea, then, becomes stored in memory and treated as though it were part of the original set. Bransford and Franks argue that the whole idea is more efficient and easier to recall than are the individual parts. Furthermore, if the parts need to be recalled later, the wholistic idea can be used as a starting point and theme for recalling as many of the parts as you can remember.

In a study that compared recall for whole ideas versus recall for separate units of information, Sullivan (1976) found that there was no forgetting of wholistic material, even after 14 hours had passed between the original learning of the information and its subsequent recall. This indicates that by creating a wholistic idea or theme which integrates more than one idea, you can make your memory more efficient. However, because you create large chunks under one theme, you often lose some of the original details.

The implications of using schemata for handling information are twofold. They make your stories easier to tell, but your stories are not going to be completely accurate. So schemata have assets and liabilities. Their assets reside within their efficiency for organizing information. Their liabilities lie in the resulting incorrect inferences.

Logical and Pragmatic Implications

When you share ideas with someone, using your schemata to organize your recall, what forms do your inferences take? Operating under the assumption that HIP involves inferential thinking, various researchers have identified two kinds of inferences: logical implications and pragmatic implications.

Rather than offer a definition of each, let me illustrate their differences through an example. Suppose you and I meet in my office, and I say to you, "Please, close the door so that we can talk." My statement not only has content, but it has implications. A *logical implication* is that the door is, in fact, open. A *pragmatic implication* might be that it is noisy outside or that I desire privacy. Either implication must be inferred by the listener. With the logical implication, the listener assumes certain things must follow if the original sentence is correct. Thus, if I ask you to close the door, it must be open. But what about the pragmatic implications? Does my request mean that it is noisy outside or that I want privacy? Are those necessary conditions for me to utter such a statement? No. Pragmatic implications are based on what is probable, not on what is necessary. People apparently have a great facility for making inferences in human interaction. Making inferences is often so subtle that you don't realize you are doing it, as the following study shows.

Brewer and Lichtenstein (1975), working with a group of students at the University of Illinois, concluded from their data that people *voluntarily* make both logical and pragmatic inferences. Furthermore, they do not remember doing so when asked about it later. Information that began as inferences (implications) became facts later on. The importance of this study is not in the fact that people make inferences. That is natural. But people take those inferences and elevate them to facts without realizing it. How much of your own knowledge started out as inferential but is now seen by you as factual? The possibility of this is rather frightening.

To illustrate the predominance of pragmatic implications even more, data from Harris and Monaco (1978) show that "several recent studies . . . have demonstrated that subjects are very likely to remember a pragmatic implication of an utterance rather than the utterance itself . . ." (p. 7). For instance, when subjects are given sentences such as:

1. The angry rioter threw a rock at the window, or
2. The hungry python caught the mouse;

the subjects are likely to recall these sentences as:

3. The angry rioter threw a rock through the window, and
4. The hungry python ate the mouse.

Although, at first, they appear similar, a closer inspection of sentences 1 and 3, and 2 and 4 will reveal a change in each. The important point is that the subjects reported later that they were given sentences 3 and 4. In fact, sentences 3 and 4 often *replaced* 1 and 2 in the minds of the subjects.

Making inferences that result in pragmatic implications is so natural that people have trouble avoiding them. This was demonstrated in a study in which people were given specific training designed to remove the tendency to make inferences (Harris, Teske, and Ginns 1975). Even with this training, the researchers found that people still made inferences when tested on mock courtroom testimony: "Subjects generally remembered both implications and assertions as definite fact, even when specifically warned not to do so" (p. 94).

Let's review the implication research. There are two kinds of implications: logical and pragmatic. Both kinds are inferences. Logical implications are inferences that must be true. Pragmatic implications are inferences that may be true, but you really don't know for sure. Whenever you create whole stories as you speak, you unknowingly include both kinds of implications. These inferences are derived from your schemata, and they help "round out" your ideas. Communicated messages contain both facts and inferences, but both are necessary for producing sensible speech.

The implications of implications should now be obvious. If you find it difficult to avoid inferences, and if you don't realize that you are making inferences, how reliable will your testimony be, for example, in a court of law? Clearly, it is questionable. Recall is rarely 100 percent accurate—there is always some distortion. The important point is not in that you treat inferences as facts, but in the probability that the inferences are true or false. As long as your inferences are true, you are all right. When they are false and you don't know it, you've got problems.

SUMMARY

Let's fit all this information about speaking into a schema for your understanding of this chapter. Most of your daily communication behavior is comprised of spontaneous speech. While interacting with others, you rely on your ability to coordinate your knowledge of the language rules with your knowledge of the social speech rules to express your intended meaning. In doing so, you lean on your memory to reconstruct or paraphrase what you want to communicate. You plan what you say as you go along and correct it through self-feedback. This produces rather short sentences which employ a limited vocabulary to express a broad range of meanings. In the process, you often make inferences without knowing it. You make not only logical inferences, you make pragmatic ones as well. The inferences (implications) often get elevated to facts when you report them later. Consequently, speaking is likened (loosely) to storytelling. You lace together facts and inferences to communicate a meaningful whole idea that the listener can understand.

SUMMARY PROPOSITIONS

1. Spontaneous speech is the act of creating your words and sentences at the time you are speaking.

2. Spontaneous speech assumes that you simultaneously engage:
   a.   language rules.
   b.   social speech rules.
   c.   semantic memory.
3. We plan our speech in terms of phrases rather than whole sentences.
4. Natural speech output is relatively simple and short and has an occasional non-fluency.
5. Unlike writing, natural speech is tattered with interruptions, pauses, and re-starts.
6. Producing natural speech uses the strategies of paraphrasing and schemata.
7. Paraphrasing is recalling information from memory, then reconstructing it for expression.
8. The most efficient way to paraphrase memory into speech is to organize your thoughts around the verb.
9. Schemata are the internal understandings that you have about concepts.
10. You use your schemata to help reconstruct what you know about the topic being discussed.
11. You use schemata to comprehend, store, and retrieve information.
12. During reconstruction for recall, you make inferences.
13. There are two kinds of inferences—logical implications and pragmatic implications.
14. Both facts and inferences are a part of producing natural speech.

EPILOGUE

We have come to the end of this book. I enjoyed writing it, and I hope you enjoyed reading it. As I wrote it, I envisioned the reader to be someone interested in knowing more about his or her ability to process information. Some critics might find the book "thin" in scientific documentation; but I have not assumed that my readers are trained in experimental psychology or research methods in communication. I have, therefore, prepared the book to be sufficiently valid in its documentation but not overburdened with footnotes and references, and therefore still fun to read. Furthermore, I have strongly resisted the temptation to write an intrapersonal text focused solely on the self-concept. To me, intrapersonal communication is much more, as my model demonstrates. But I also hope that you see yourself in this book, as I see myself.

What I have attempted to do is to take some of the most important findings in information processing and apply them to intrapersonal communication. The core activity of human communication is processing information, whether in your head or in a conversation. I hope you have come to appreciate my attempt to model intrapersonal communication so that it includes HIP and its surrounding components (cognitive, affective, and operational). A person who grasps these elements is beginning to understand intrapersonal communication.

From time to time, people ask me about the "best book" to read on HIP, one that is not too technical and laden with experimental procedures. I hope this book answers those requirements. But for those of you who wish to pursue this area further, I would strongly recommend two texts. Both can be easily understood by people whose training is not in psychology.

The first is Frank Smith's *Comprehension and Learning* (Holt, Rinehart & Winston, 1975). Smith is a psychologist in the Canadian tradition, which means that he is not always in the laboratory conducting experiments. His book is fun to read. It was written for teachers (and prospective teachers), but it is of interest to anyone wanting to know more about how humans come to know. Many ideas that he has developed about HIP came directly from his own research in the reading process.

The second book I recommend is Ulric Neisser's *Cognition and Reality* (W. H. Freeman, 1976). This is an enjoyable book to read. Neisser (like Smith) is willing to speculate in order to generate new ideas about HIP. Perhaps more than any other American psychologist, Neisser is one of the most thought-provoking writers in cognitive research. For those of you who are interested in the human brain, there is an inexpensive paperback called *Inside the Brain* (Mentor, 1980) by William Calvin and George Ojemann, which is easy to read and available in local bookstores.

Finally, I should comment on the "applicability" of the material covered in this text. Everyone reading this book should have developed insights about his or her own

HIP skills, and if that is all you get from reading this text, I'm satisfied. Some of you, however, may be looking for ways to apply this material to your daily life. Exactly how you do that is up to you. But there is nothing more practical than an improved understanding of the thing you are studying. For instance, the more you know about how a car runs, the better off you will be when it comes time to adjust the carburetor, or to evaluate a mechanic's recommendation that you need a valve job at only 12,000 miles. Likewise, if you understand such concepts as dual coding, you can take advantage of this phenomenon when studying important information. For instance, on the night before an exam, you might try reading your notes aloud instead of silently rehearsing them. Seeing and hearing your notes will produce dual coding. How would you apply your understanding of logical and pragmatic implications? An understanding of all kinds of inferences should produce in you a more critical attitude about what you say and what others say to you. If you expect errors in what people say, you won't be too surprised or disappointed when they occur.

   Suffice it to say that this material is easy to apply if you understand it well and are willing to envision how it can affect your life.

APPENDIX

TAKING NOTES AND STUDYING FOR EXAMS

Taking Notes

The success you have in school typically hinges on your skills at taking notes. Some students try to record every word in a lecture, and because writing is the slowest form of communication, they miss important points. Unless you know shorthand of some kind, it will be impossible for you to record any lecture word-for-word.

Note-taking is a special listening skill. If you approach taking notes using the following suggestions you should find that you will get all you need from a lecture.

1. Remember, note-taking is just that. It is not recording. Taking notes involves paraphrasing. It means that you translate what the instructor is saying into words that are meaningful to you. You should try to use the terms that the teacher uses, but you should not attempt to parrot the lecture.

2. Look for structure. Listen for deliberate pauses in your instructor's voice. They often note that the last point should be written down. If the instructor writes something on the board, copy it. He or she does so to make it easier for you to take notes. Most lectures are not continuous stories with only one beginning and one end. Look for beginnings and ends. Outline the lecture in the same way you would prepare a speech; use roman numerals, upper and lower case letters, and indented subpoints. It is a good idea to type your notes after you leave class. This helps you learn, while giving you an opportunity to fill in gaps with information you recall at this time.

3. Trust your memory. Your notes represent cues for recall; they do not represent all that was said. If you are paying attention and actively listening, your notes should provide cues for your memory. What you have written down is not all that you should be able to say when it is time for an exam. Your memory will work for you, if you provide the right key words.

4. Your notes will not be the same as someone else's. If you miss a class, get notes from at least two people, then construct the best set of notes that you can from both of them. Borrow notes from people who are doing well in class. That they are getting good grades may mean that they are taking good notes.

Studying for Exams

The first prerequisite for doing well on exams is that you have all the necessary information available to you for taking the exam. Missing material will hurt you. If you have been faithful in class attendance, have actively listened, have read the assigned materials, and have taken good notes, then you have the basic material from which to study.

People's performance on exams is mainly a function of their study habits. Unless you are particularly gifted, you will need to review the material before you enter class on exam day. You should study several times rather than "cramming" just once. We know from research that if a person is under stress, it is more difficult to learn material than it is to rehearse it. So, make sure that you at least understand the material, then all you will have to do is rehearse it.

1.   With each review of the material, try to provide more and more structure. If possible, reduce information into smaller units, such as making up words out of the first letters in a list. Don't simply reread; this only takes time. You should make outlines. You should underline and highlight the material to make it stand out. As with the lecture, you will not be able to memorize every word in your notes. So build structures and memorize them.

2.   When rehearsing material, start in a different place each time (unless the chronology is part of the exam). By doing this you will avoid overlearning some material while underlearning other material. The primacy-recency effect shows that people tend to remember the first and last items in a set of materials. The middle material is often forgotten. By altering your starting points, you give all sections a chance at being first or last.

3.   Take time to study. Start at least a week in advance. Plan to set aside time each day for review. Cramming everything is very tiring and anxiety producing. Cramming may be useful, especially just before exam time, but you should be cramming your restructured notes. If you are cramming to learn unfamiliar material, and not to memorize your rehearsed notes, you will most likely have problems during exams.

REFERENCES

PART 1: SOME BASICS

Chapter 1: Perceiving Information

Boulding, K. 1956. *The Image*. Ann Arbor, MI: Univ. of Michigan Press.

Carmichael, L.; Hogan, H.; and Walter, A. 1932. An Experimental Study of the Effect of Language on the Reproduction of Visually Perceived Form. *J. Exp. Psychol.* 15:73–86.

Miller, G. 1968. Human Information Processing: Some Research Guidelines. In *Conceptual Frontiers in Speech Communication*, ed. R. Kibler and L. Barker. New York: Speech Communication Ass.

Neisser, U. 1976. *Cognition and Reality*. San Francisco: W. H. Freeman & Co.

Smith, F. 1975. *Comprehension and Learning*. New York: Holt, Rinehart & Winston, Inc.

Chapter 2: Necessary Equipment

Anderson, P.; Garrison, J.; and Anderson, J. 1979. Implication of a Neurophysiological Approach for the Study of Nonverbal Communication. *Hum. Commun. Res.* 6:74–89.

Bartlett, F. 1932. *Remembering*. Cambridge, England: Cambridge Univ. Press.

Calvin, W. H., and Ojemann, G. A. 1980. *Inside the Brain*. New York: Mentor.

Coon, D. 1977. *Introduction to Psychology*. St. Paul, MN: West Publishing Co.

Geschwind, N. 1970. Language and the Brain. *Science* 170:940–47.

Laughery, K., and Fell, J. 1969. Subject Preferences and the Nature of Information Storage in STM. *J. Exp. Psychol.* 82:193–97.

Lennenberg, E. 1967. *Biological Foundations of Language*. New York: John Wiley & Sons, Inc.

Moscovitch, M. 1976. On the Representation of Language in the Right Hemisphere of Right-Handed People. *Brain and Language* 3:47–71.

Nathan, P. 1969. *The Nervous System*. Philadelphia: J. B. Lippincott Co.

PART 2: HUMAN INFORMATION PROCESSING

Chapter 3: Gathering Information

Cherry, C. 1953. Some Experiments on the Recognition of Speech with One and Two Ears. *J. Acoust. Soc. Am.* 25:975–79.

Cherry, C. 1978. *On Human Communication*. Cambridge, MA: MIT Press.

Craik, F., and Lockhart, R. 1972. Levels of Processing: A Framework for Memory Research. *J. Verb. Learn. Verb. Behav.* 11:671–84.

Neisser, U. 1967. *Cognitive Psychology*. New York: Appleton-Century-Crofts.

Neisser, U. 1976. *Cognition and Reality*. San Francisco: W. H. Freeman & Co.

Norman, D. 1969. *Memory and Attention*. New York: John Wiley & Sons, Inc.

Chapter 4: Storing and Retrieving Information

Allport, G., and Postman, L. 1945. The Basic Psychology of Rumor. *Trans. N. Y. Acad. Sci.* series 2, 8:61–81.

Jenkins, J., and Dallenbach, K. 1924. Obliviscence during Sleep and Waking. *Am. J. Psychol.* 35:605–12.

Miller, G. 1956. The Magical Number Seven, Plus or Minus Two: Some Limits on Our Capacity for Processing Information. *Psychol. Rev.* 63:81–97.

Rosnow, R. 1966. What Happened to the Law of Primacy? *J. Commun.* 16:10–31.

Tulving, E. 1972. Episodic and Semantic Memory. In *Organization of Memory*, ed. E. Tulving and W. Donaldson. New York: Academic Press, Inc.

Tulving, E., and Osler, S. 1968. Effectiveness of Retrieval Cues in Memory for Words. *J. Exp. Psychol.* 77:593–601.

Underwood, B. 1957. Interference and Forgetting. *Psychol. Rev.* 64:49–60.

Waugh, N., and Norman, D. 1965. Primary Memory. *Psychol. Rev.* 72:89–104.

Wickelgren, W. 1965. Acoustic Similarity and Intrusion Errors in Short-Term Memory. *J. Exp. Psychol.* 70:102–108.

Wicken, D., and Clark, S. 1968. Osgood Dimensions as an Encoding Class in Short-Term Memory. *J. Exp. Psychol.* 78:580–84.

PART 3: COGNITIVE COMPONENT

Chapter 5: Meaning

Anderson, J., and Bower, G. H. 1973. *Human Associative Memory*. Washington, DC: V. H. Winston & Sons.

Bruner, J. 1964. The Course of Cognitive Growth, *Am. Psychol.* 19:1–15.

Collins, A. M., and Loftus, E. F. 1975. A Spreading Activation Theory of Semantic Processing. *Psychol. Rev.* 82:407–28.

Cohen, G. 1977. *The Psychology of Cognition*. London: Academic Press, Inc.

Olson, D. 1970. Language and Thought: Aspects of a Cognitive Theory of Semantics. *Psychol. Rev.* 77:257–73.

Rosch, E. 1975. Cognitive Representations of Semantic Categories. *J. Exp. Psychol.* 104:192–233.

Rumelhart, D. E.; Lindsey, P. H.; and Norman, D. A. 1972. A Process Model for Long Term Memory. In *Organization of Memory*, ed. E. Tulving and W. Donaldson. New York: Academic Press, Inc.

Schlesinger, I. M. 1977. *Production and Comprehension of Utterances*. Hillsdale, NJ: Lawrence Erlbaum Assocs., Inc.

Smith, F. 1975. *Comprehension and Learning*. New York: Holt, Rinehart & Winston, Inc.

Chapter 6: Language

Fraser, C.; Bellugi, U.; and Brown, R. 1963. Control of Grammar in Imitation, Comprehension and Production. *J. Verb. Learn. Verb. Behav.* 2:121–35.

Knapp, M.; Wieman, J.; and Daly, J. 1978. Nonverbal Communication: Issues and Appraisal. *Hum. Commun. Res.* 4:271–80.

Kosslyn, S. 1975. Information Representation in Visual Images. *Cognitive Psychol.* 7:341–70.

Shatz, C. 1978. On the Development of Communicative Understandings: An Early Strategy for Interpreting and Responding to Messages. *Cognitive Psychol.* 10:271–301.

Slobin, D. 1979. *Psycholinguistics.* 2nd ed. Glenview, IL: Scott, Foresman & Co.

Taylor, I. 1976. *Introduction to Psycholinguistics.* New York: Holt, Rinehart & Winston, Inc.

PART 4: AFFECTIVE COMPONENT

Chapter 7: Attitudes and Self-Concept

Berscheid, E., and Walster, E. 1969. *Interpersonal Attraction.* Reading, MA: Addison-Wesley Publishing Co., Inc.

Bugelski, B. R. 1973. *An Introduction to the Principles of Psychology.* Indianapolis: Bobbs-Merrill Co., Inc.

Burgoon, M., and Ruffner, M. 1978. *Human Communication.* New York: Holt, Rinehart & Winston, Inc.

Goss, B.; Olds, S.; and Thompson, M. 1978. Behavioral Support for Systematic Desensitization for Communication Apprehension. *Hum. Commun. Res.* 4:158–63.

Maehr, M.; Mensing, J.; and Nafzgher, S. 1962. Concept of Self and the Reactions of Others. *Sociometry* 25:353–57.

McCroskey, J., and Wheeless, L. 1976. *Introduction to Human Communication.* Boston: Allyn & Bacon, Inc.

Powers, W.; Jordan, W.; and Street, R. 1979. Language Indices in the Measurement of Cognitive Complexity: Is Complexity Loquacity? *Hum. Commun. Res.* 6:69–73.

Rokeach, M. 1968. *Beliefs, Attitudes and Values.* San Francisco: Jossey-Bass Inc., Pubs.

Rosenberg, M. 1968. Discussion: The Concept of Self. In *Theories of Cognitive Consistency: A Source-Book*, ed. R. Abelson et al. Chicago: Rand McNally & Co.

Saine, T. 1976. Cognitive Complexity, Affective Stimulus Valence, and Information Transmission. *Hum. Commun. Res.* 2:281–88.

Chapter 8: Consistency Theories

Brehm, J., and Cohen, A. 1962. *Explorations in Cognitive Dissonance.* New York: John Wiley & Sons, Inc.

Feather, N. 1967. A Structural Balance Approach to the Analysis of Communication Effects. In *Advances in Experimental Social Psychology*, ed. L. Berkowitz, vol. 3. New York: Academic Press, Inc.

Festinger, L. 1957. *A Theory of Cognitive Dissonance.* Stanford, CA: Stanford Univ. Press.

Festinger, L., and Carlsmith, J. 1959. Cognitive Consequences of Forced Compliance. *J. Abnorm. Soc. Psychol.* 58:203–10.

Freedman, J., and Sears, D. 1966. Selective Exposure. In *Advances in Experimental Social Psychology,* ed. L. Berkowitz, vol. 3. New York: Academic Press, Inc.

Greenwald, A., and Ronis, D. 1978. Twenty Years of Cognitive Dissonance: Case Study of the Evolution of a Theory. *Psychol. Rev.* 85:53–57.

Heider, F. 1946. Attitudes and Cognitive Organizations. *J. Psychol.* 21:107–12.

Heider, F. 1958. *The Psychology of Interpersonal Relations.* New York: John Wiley & Sons, Inc.

Jordan, N. 1953. Behaviorial Forces That Are a Function of Attitudes and of Cognitive Organization. *Hum. Relat.* 6:273–87.

Mills, J. 1966. Interest in Supporting and Discrepant Information. In *Cognitive Consistency,* ed. S. Feldman. New York: Academic Press, Inc.

Osgood, C., and Tannenbaum, P. 1955. The Principle of Congruity in the Prediction of Attitude Change. *Psychol. Rev.* 62:42–55.

Zajonc, R. 1968. Cognitive Theories of Social Behavior. In *Handbook of Social Psychology,* ed. G. Lindzey and E. Aronson, vol. 1. Reading, MA: Addison-Wesley Publishing Co., Inc.

PART 5: OPERATIONAL COMPONENT

Chapter 9: Listening

Aronson, D. 1974. Stimulus Factors and Listening Strategies in Auditory Memory: A Theoretical Analysis. *Cognitive Psychol.* 6:108–32.

Black, J.; Turner, T.; and Bower, G. 1979. Point of View in Narrative Comprehension, Memory, and Production. *J. Verb. Learn. Verb. Behav.* 18:187–98.

Bryant, J., and Comisky, P. 1978. The Effect of Positioning a Message within Differentially Cognitively Involving Portions of a Television Segment on Recall of the Message. *Hum. Commun. Res.* 5:63–75.

Cherry, C. 1953. Some Experiments on the Recognition of Speech, with One and Two Ears. *J. Acoust. Soc. Am.* 25:975–79.

Cole, R., and Jakimik, J. 1978. Understanding Speech: How Words Are Heard. In *Strategies of Information Processing,* ed. G. Underwood. London: Academic Press, Inc.

Eimas, P. 1974. Auditory and Linguistic Processing of Cues for Place of Articulation by Infants. *Percept. Psychophys.* 16:513–21.

Garner, W. R. 1974. *The Processing of Information and Structure.* Hillsdale, NJ: 1958. Lawrence Erlbaum Assocs., Inc.

Green, R. T. 1958. The Attention-getting Value of Structural Change. *Br. J. of Psychol.* 49:311–14.

Horowitz, M., and Berkowitz, A. 1967. Listening and Reading, Speaking and Writing: An Experimental Investigation of Differential Acquisition and Reproduction of Memory. *Percept. Mot. Skills* 24:207–15.

Hulse, S.; Deese, J.; and Egeth, H. 1975. *The Psychology of Learning.* New York: McGraw-Hill Book Co.

Liberman, P. 1972. *Speech Acoustics and Perception.* Indianapolis: Bobbs-Merrill Co., Inc.

Liberman, P.; Mattingly, I.; and Turvey, M. 1972. Language Codes and Memory

Codes. In *Coding Processes in Human Memory*, ed. A. Melton and E. Martin. Washington, DC: V. H. Winston & Sons.

Neisser, U. 1976. *Cognition and Reality*. San Francisco: W. H. Freeman & Co.

Newman, S., and Saltz, E. 1958. Isolation Effects: Stimulus and Response Generalization as Explanatory Concepts. *J. Exp. Psychol.* 55:467–72.

Orr, D. 1968. Time Compressed Speech—A Perspective. *J. Commun.* 18:288–92.

Taylor, W. 1956. Recent Development in the Use of Cloze Procedure. *Journalism Q.* 33:426–99.

Walker, L. 1975–76. Comprehending Writing and Spontaneous Speech. *Reading Research Q.* 11:144–67.

Chapter 10: Speaking

Bartlett, F. 1932. *Remembering*. Cambridge, England: Cambridge Univ. Press.

Bransford, J., and Franks, J. 1971. The Abstraction of Linguistic Ideas. *Cognitive Psychol.* 2:331–50.

Brewer, W., and Lichtenstein, E. 1975. Recall of Logical and Pragmatic Implications in Sentences with Dichotomous and Continuous Antonyms. *Mem. Cognition* 3:315–18.

Bruner, J. 1973. *Beyond the Information Given: Studies in Psychology and Knowing*. New York: W. W. Norton & Co., Inc.

Deese, J. 1978. Thought into Speech. *Am. Sci.* 66:314–21.

Giles, H., and Powesland, P. 1975. *Speech Style and Social Evaluation*. London: Academic Press, Inc.

Giles, H., and St. Clair, R. 1979. *Language and Social Psychology*. Baltimore: University Park Press.

Harris, R., and Monaco, G. 1978. Psychology of Pragmatic Implication: Information Processing between the Lines. *J. Psychol.: General* 107:1–27.

Harris, R.; Teske, R.; and Ginns, M. 1975. Memory for Pragmatic Implications from Courtroom Testimony. *Bull. Psychol. Soc.* 6:494–96.

Housel, T. J. 1981. Conversational Message Processing: A Schema Theory Approach. A paper presented to the International Communication Association, Minneapolis, May 1981.

Liberman, P.; Mattingly, I.; and Turvey, M. 1972. Language Codes and Memory Codes. In *Coding Processes in Human Memory*, ed. A. Melton and E. Martin. Washington, DC: V. H. Winston & Sons.

Lindsley, J. 1975. Producing Simple Utterances: How Far Ahead Do We Plan? *Cognitive Psychol.* 7:1–19.

Loftus, J., and Palmer, J. 1974. Reconstruction of Automobile Destruction: An Example of the Interaction between Language and Memory. *J. Verb. Learn. Verb. Behav.* 13:585–89.

Miller, G., and Hewgill, M. 1964. The Effects of Variations in Nonfluency on Audience Ratings of Source Credibility. *Q. J. Speech* 50:36–44.

Nathan, P. 1969. *The Nervous System*. Philadelphia: J. B. Lippincott Co.

Rumelhart, D., and Ortony, A. 1977. The Representation of Knowledge in Memory. In *Schooling and the Acquisition of Knowledge*, ed. R. Anderson, R. Spiro, and W. Montague. Hillsdale, NJ: Lawrence Erlbaum Assocs., Inc.

Smith, F. 1975. *Comprehension and Learning*. New York: Holt, Rinehart & Winston, Inc.

Sullivan, M. 1976. The Effects of Wakefulness and Sleep on the Memory for Complex Linguistic Ideas. Ph.D. Dissertation, Univ. of Colorado.

Yates, A. 1963. Delayed Auditory Feedback. *Psychol. Bull.* 60:213–32.

GLOSSARY

accessibility   The ease with which items can be retrieved from long-term memory.

affective component   Part of the intrapersonal processes of communication. Includes values—attitudes—beliefs and self-concept.

affective meaning   One of the three parts to meaning. Often called connotative meaning, it refers to feelings people associate with words.

assimilation   One of the ways we distort information as we communicate. It means making a story fit your attitudes and knowledge.

associates   Words that are closely associated with each other in people's minds.

associations   How words and ideas are learned and stored in memory such that the thought of one leads to another.

association areas   Portions of the human brain where ideas are stored and where relations between ideas form.

attention   Removing distractions and devoting energy toward perceiving a message.

attitudes   Our predispositions to respond in an evaluative way to objects, people, and ideas.

auditory capacity   The amount of information that the ears can handle.

auditory information   Sensations sent to the brain from the ears.

balance theory   One of the consistency theories. Its premise is that people strive to maintain harmony in their feelings and perceptions.

beliefs   Those things about the world you think are true.

brain   The interpretation center for HIP. The brain interprets the signals sent by the receptors (ears, eyes, nose, etc.).

cerebral cortex   The largest part of the human brain. The cerebral cortex has two halves and stores information received by the brain. It is the location of our memories.

cerebral lateralization   Refers to the belief that each half of the brain has primary responsibilities. The left side is considered the verbal side, while the right side is thought to be our nonverbal side.

chunking   How information is organized and grouped in STM. Chunks are a number of inputs grouped together mentally to be treated as larger units.

class inclusion   Part of formal meaning. It refers to the fact that things can be defined as members of some group, such as, a cat is an animal. Its shorthand notation is ISA.

closure   One of our natural tendencies in perception. We tend to complete any figure that is incomplete. We fill in missing details.

codability   The ease with which an input may be meaningfully translated into something you already understand.

coding   Translating a signal from one form into another. For instance, we use the alphabet to translate spoken words into written words.

cognitive complexity   Your ability to handle a lot of information at one time. People differ in how cognitively complex they are.

cognitive component   Part of the intrapersonal processes of communication. It includes meaning and language.

cognitive pause   A natural hesitation in the flow of speech to think about what you have said or are going to say.

communication   Exchanging verbal and nonverbal messages for the purpose of provoking meaning in each other's minds.

communication competence   Your ability to interact with others on both the verbal and nonverbal levels of communication.

congruity theory   One of the consistency theories. It suggests that people adjust any inconsistent ideas to more closely coincide with each other.

connotation   Part of the affective aspect of meaning. It refers to your feelings and attitudes about the topic in question.

consistency   The key organizing principle of the mind. We maintain in our minds ideas, attitudes, and meanings in such a way that there are minimal conflicts. Inconsistency means that one idea contradicts another idea.

conversation   A sequence of paraphrased ideas that is brought about by our interaction.

corpus callosum   Fibers that connect the left and right hemispheres of the brain.

cued recall   The kind of remembering wherein someone gives you a hint to help you recall the information.

decay   The belief that some information in memory fades away because it is not used often enough or was not well learned to begin with.

decoding   Translating what you hear and see into the appropriate meanings. In verbal communication, it refers to listening and reading.

DEDE   A shorthand notation that stands for decode-encode-decode-encode.

denotation   Our understanding of the formal and functional aspects of the meaning we have for a particular word. It is similar to a dictionary meaning.

depth of processing   How thoroughly you analyze an input. Noise requires the least amount of processing; important information requires the most.

dissonance theory   One of the consistency theories. It emphasizes how we justify our attitudes and behaviors.

DOESA   A shorthand notation to represent the functional aspect of meaning.

dual coding   Occurs when information is stored both auditorily and visually, thus increasing the likelihood that a unit of information will be remembered.

enactive representation   Having something stored in memory according to its associated actions. Knowing how to skip rope is enactively represented in memory.

encoding   Coding your meanings into words, sentences, gestures. In verbal communication, it refers to speaking and writing.

episodic LTM   One of the ways information can be stored in LTM. Information is stored according to a sequence of events that make up a whole "story." What you did last year on vacation would be stored as an episode in LTM.

expressive capabilities   Your abilities to speak, write, and use nonverbal communication. Its counterpart is receptive capability.

external information   Information provided by the world around you. In communication, messages from others are external information.

familiarity   One of the perceptual tendencies. It refers to the way in which we interpret input to coincide with things we already know. We look for things that we are familiar with.

forgetting   Not being able to recall something out of memory. Whether things are temporarily forgotten or permanently lost is still unknown at this time.

formal meaning   One of the three parts of meaning. Also called denotative meaning, it refers to our understanding of what something is and what attributes it has. It includes class inclusion and property relations.

functional meaning   One of the three parts of meaning. It refers to our understanding of what something does or how it is used.

gathering information   One of the three stages of basic HIP. It includes how we sense, how we attend to, and how we perceive incoming information.

grammatical pause   A natural hesitation in the flow of speech that indicates the end of a clause, sentence, or idea. It is the way we punctuate speech.

HASA   A shorthand notation to represent the property relations inherent in formal meaning.

hearing   Receiving auditory inputs.

hemispheres   The respective halves of the cerebral cortex of the human brain.

HIP   An abbreviation for human information processing. It includes gathering, storing, and retrieving information.

homeostasis   Striving to maintain relative harmony or balance among our ideas, attitudes, and meanings. Similar to consistency.

iconic representation   Stored visualizations.

image   A term used by Kenneth Boulding (1956) to refer to knowledge, ideas, and meanings that we develop over time.

information   Any input that a person attends to for the purposes of reducing uncertainty or confirming prior knowledge.

information overload   Having more information confronting you than you can handle at one time.

information underload   Not having enough information to keep you busy.

I/N ratio   Information divided by noise. It refers to how you cope with a barrage of data at one time. The less you have classified as information, compared with the amount you have classified as noise, the more focused your attention.

interference   Other information that causes you to forget something because you get confused or develop a block.

internal information   Information that emanates from within you. Your memories, expectations, knowledge, feelings, and biases all contribute to internal information.

interpersonal   Means "between people," in contrast to intrapersonal. For instance, interpersonal communication involves communication between at least two people.

intrapersonal   Means "within people," in contrast to interpersonal. This book is about the intrapersonal processes that allow you to communicate.

ISA A shorthand notation to represent the class inclusion part of formal meaning.

kinesics Part of nonverbal communication. This refers to how you use your body to communicate, with things such as gestures, facial expressions, and eye contact.

language Communication through words and sentences. Language is the verbal system we use to communicate.

language competence Your understanding of the language rules that allows you to express the meanings you have stored in memory.

language learning The way you learn to use language to communicate. It consists of inferring the rules of language, then testing them to see whether they work.

language performance The counterpart to language competence. It refers to actual sentences that you produce as you communicate.

leveling One of the ways we distort information as we communicate. It refers to making the story shorter and simpler by omitting some of the original information.

listening Perceiving what we hear.

listening comprehension How much we remember and understand from what we hear.

logical implication An inference made that it is certain—it must be true, given prior information. Its counterpart is the pragmatic implication.

LTM An abbreviation for long-term memory. LTM is our permanent record of experiences.

meaning Your understanding of the formal, functional, and affective aspects of a word or concept.

meaningfulness The ease with which you can understand a particular message. Incoming ideas are more meaningful if you can immediately assign meaning to them.

message distortion The act of changing information as you communicate about it to someone else. We typically distort information through leveling, sharpening, and assimilation.

neurons The nerve cells in the brain that conduct the electrical–chemical impulses that carry information.

noise Inputs and sensations that you do not classify as information. You just monitor noise; you don't concentrate on it.

noncued recall The kind of remembering wherein you must provide both the structure and the content of the recalled information. It is contrasted with cued recall.

nonfluencies Disruptions in speech, such as "ah," "uh," or repetitions or restarts.

nonverbal information Messages that come to you through means other than verbal. Paralanguage (tone of voice) and kinesics (bodily movements) comprise a large part of nonverbal information.

occipital lobe An area in the back part of the cerebral cortex where visual information is processed.

operational component Part of the intrapersonal processes of communication. It includes listening and speaking.

overgeneralization Using a rule of language in too many different instances, thus creating incorrect expressions.

paralanguage How we communicate through our vocal characteristics of pitch, loudness, and timbre. Paralanguage is part of nonverbal information.

paraphrasing Recalling information in a reconstructive way. It is piecing together information that you recall to communicate with someone else.

pattern recognition A very rapid process of perception that allows initial recognition of the defining features of any input.

percept A mental image or idea produced through the process of perception.

perception Interpreting your sensations. Perception = sensations + meanings + feelings.

peripheral vision Being able to see things on both sides of your field of vision while you are looking straight ahead.

persuasion Communication designed to either reinforce or change your attitudes.

phonology The study of phonemes, or how people structure sounds to begin forming words.

pragmatic implication An inference made that is probabilistic — it is not necessarily true. Its counterpart is the logical implication.

primacy-recency Remembering the earlier and later items in a story more than you remember those items in between.

proactive interference Forgetting that is caused by prior learning interfering with current learning. It occurs when what you learned before hinders what you are trying to learn now. It is the opposite of retroactive interference.

property relations Part of formal meaning. It refers to the attributes that you see things as having; for instance, a canary has yellow feathers. Its notation is HASA.

psycho-logic An informal system of logic that underlies consistency. Unlike formal logic, psycho-logic is only required to "make sense."

rambling recall The act of sharing with someone what you remember, but doing so in a disorganized manner that is embellished with new details.

reading comprehension How much we remember and understand from what we read.

receptive capabilities Your abilities to listen, read, and understand nonverbal communication. Its counterpart is expressive capabilities.

recognition The kind of remembering wherein you are given a group of options from which to choose the "right" answer. Recognition memory occurs when you realize that what you hear and see matches what you already know.

reconstructive recall Piecing together a number of items from LTM as you recall an idea or event.

redundancy The inherent predictability of our usage of language.

rehearsal Repeating information to yourself so that you increase the likelihood of remembering it later.

retrieving information Conducting a memory search to reconstruct what you have stored in memory.

retroactive interference The opposite of proactive interference. This occurs when new learning causes you to forget material you learned earlier.

schemata Bundles of knowledge stored in memory that serve to represent all we know about any particular topic. (Schema is the singular form of schemata.)

selective attention Choosing to pay attention to only a portion of all the available inputs at one time.

selective perception Interpreting what you hear and see according to your biases and expectations.

selective recall   Retrieving out of memory only a portion of all that you know about something.

self-concept   Your attitude about you as a person; how you see yourself in terms of attributes and roles.

self-feedback   Monitoring and correcting your own speech behavior.

self-fulfilling prophecy   Letting our labels dominate our expectations and vice versa. People who expect to lose, increase the likelihood that they will lose. How you label something often determines how you see it.

semantic LTM   One of the ways long-term memory is organized. Meanings are stored in semantic memory.

semantics   Meanings you have stored for the words you use.

sensation   The response from our receptors telling us that our senses have detected a signal.

sharpening   One of the ways we distort information as we communicate. It is taking a few details and making them more important than they were in the original story.

speaking rate   How fast people speak, typically measured by words per minute.

speech   Vocalized language sounds designed to communicate.

speech perception   Our ability to detect, recognize, and interpret speech signals.

spontaneous speech   Making up your sentences as you talk.

STM   An abbreviation for short-term memory. STM is a temporary "working" memory designed to hold current information in place until we use it or store it in LTM.

storing information   The second part of basic HIP. It includes both STM and LTM.

symbolic representation   Having something stored in memory according to its appropriate signs or symbols. Words are symbolically represented in memory.

syntax   The way you organize words into sentences to conform to proper grammatical rules.

temporal lobe   Part of the cerebral cortex of the brain where language and speech functions originate.

unit relationship   In the balance triangles, the relationship between two people or ideas that go together regularly and do affect one another.

universals   Recurring patterns of language learning that occur regardless of the language being learned or the culture within which the language is being learned.

usage   How people regularly construct sentences to express what they mean.

VAB system   A shorthand notation that refers to your internal values (V), attitudes (A), and beliefs (B). The VAB system is part of the affective component.

values   The core of our internal system of values, attitudes, and beliefs. They represent the most fundamental standards of life that we adhere to.

visual capacity   The amount of information that the eyes can handle.

visual information   Sensations sent to the brain from the eye.

INDEX

Accessibility, 35
Affective
  component of intrapersonal
    processes of communication, 4,
    67–86
  level of meaning, 46–47
Attention
  and noise, 24
  principles of, 26
  selective, 9, 25–26
Attitudes, 67–75
  and consistency, 67–69
  defined, 70
  and meaning, 46–47
Assimilation, 40
Associates, 49
Association areas of the brain, 14

Balance
  preference for, 79
  theory of consistency, 77–79
  and timing, 80
Beliefs, 70–71
Boulding's image, 5–6
Brain, 13–16

Cerebral cortex, 14–15
Cerebral lateralization, 15–16
Chunking, 34
Class inclusion, 46, 48
Closure, 6
"Cocktail party problem," 27, 91
Codability, of new information, 38
Coding, 89
Cognitive
  complexity, 73–74
  component of intrapersonal
    processes of communication, 4,
    45–63
  dissonance, 82–85

Communication. See Intrapersonal
    processes of communication;
    Language; and Nonverbal
    communication
Communication skills
  and language, 56–57
  and self-concept, 72
Comprehension, listening, 92–95
Congruity
  applications to HIP, 81–82
  theory of consistency, 80–81
Connotative meaning, 46
Corpus callosum, 15
Consistency
  and attitudes, 67–69
  theories, 77–86
Conversation, and schemata, 106
Cue, for recall, 35, 39
Cued recall, 39

Decoding, 89–90
DEDE, 89
Denotative meaning, 46
Depth of processing, 28
Dissonance
  cognitive, 82–85
  postdecisional, 83
Distortion
  of information, 18
  of messages, 40
DOESA, 46
Dual coding, 95
Dual-coding hypothesis, 38

Ears and eyes, 16–17
  ranges of, 16
  compared, 17
  coordinated inputs of, 17
Enactive representation of meaning, 50
Encoding, 89–90

Encoding specificity, 35, 39
Episodic organization, 36
Expectations, and perception, 7
External information, 5, 6, 18, 19
Eyes. *See* Ears and eyes

Familiarity, and perception, 7
Forgetting
  in LTM, 36–37
  in STM, 34
Formal level of meaning, 46–47
Free recall, 39
Functional level of meaning, 46, 47

HASA, 46
Hearing. *See* Ears and eyes
  versus listening, 90
Homeostasis, 19, 68
Human information processing (HIP)
  and congruity, 81–82
  defined, 3, 4
  and dissonance, 84–85
  and language, 55–56
  and language learning, 62
  and meaning, 45
  underlying assumptions of, 18–19
Hypothesis testing, 59

Iconic representation, 50–51
Image, 5–6
Imagery, 58–59
Implications
  logical, 107–108
  pragmatic, 107–108
Inconsistencies, 19
Inconsistency, resolving of, 84
Inferences, 106
Information
  defined, 23–24, 30
  external, 5, 6, 18, 19
  gathering of, 23–30
  internal, 5, 6
  quantity and quality of, 24
  retrieval of, 38–41
  storage of, 15, 33–38
  structuring of, 18
  utility of, 23
Information/noise ratio (I/N), 26–28,
    30, 96
Information processing
  basics of, 13
  levels of, 28
Information overload, 27, 34
Information underload, 27

Interference, 34
  proactive, 36–37
  retroactive, 36–37
Internal information, 5, 6
Interpersonal processes of
    communication, 4
Intrapersonal processes of
    communication
  affective component of, 67–86
  cognitive component of, 45–63
  defined, 3–4
  and HIP, 4
  operational component of, 89–109
ISA, 46
Item decay, 34

Kinesics, 58

Language, 55–63
  centrality of, 55–56
  and communication skills, 56–57
  and HIP, 55–56
  and LTM, 57
  universals of, 60
  and verbal associations, 49
Language competence, 56–57
Language learning, principles of, 60
Language performance, 56
Length of utterances, 101
Leveling, 40
Listening, 89–97
  compared with reading, 94–95
  comprehension, 92–95
  improving, 95–96
  requirements for, 91–92
  selectivity in, 90–91
  strategies, 93–94
  versus hearing, 90
Long-term memory (LTM), 35–37
  compared with short-term memory,
    37

Meaning, 45–52
  creation of, 51-52
  levels of, 46-47
  and natural language usage, 49–50
  organization of, 47
  and perception, 6
  and sensation, 25
Meaningfulness, of new information, 38
Meanings, as categories, 48
Memory, and the brain, 15
Message distortion, 40
Mind-set, perceptual, 29

Monitoring, of noise, 24, 27
Multichannel inputs, and new
    information, 38

Natural language usage, and meaning,
    49–50
Natural speech output, 101–103
Nervous system, 16
Neurons, 14, 15–16
Noise, 24
Noncued recall, 39
Nonfluencies, 102
Nonverbal communication, 57–59
    and the brain, 15
Nonverbal memory, 58

Occipital lobe, 14, 15
Operational component of
    intrapersonal processes of
    communication, 4, 89–109
Orderliness, 19
Organization
    in LTM, 36
    of meaning, 47–50
Organizing, and perception, 6
Overgeneralization, 60–61

Paralanguage, 58
Paraphrasing, 103
Pattern recognition, 25
Pausing, 102
Perception, 6–10, 29–30
    parts of, 29
    selective, 29
    versus sensation, 16
Perceptions
    as habits, 7–8
    and meaning, 45
Percepts, 8
Perceptual mind-set, 29
Phonology, 56
Postdecisional dissonance, 83
P–O–X triangles, 77–79
Predict–then–confirm, listening
    strategy, 94
Primacy-recency effect, 40
Proactive interference, 36–37
Property relations, 46
Psycho-logic, 68–69

Reading, compared with listening,
    94–95
Recall
    cued, 39

Recall (continued)
    free, 39
    noncued, 39
    rambling, 95
    and reconstruction, 38
    selective, 9–10
Recalling information, 38–40
Recognition
    and memory, 39
    of speech, 91–92
Reduction, of information, 18
Rehearsal
    in LTM, 38
    in STM, 33–34
Retroactive interference, 36–37

Schema(ta), 105–108
    and conversation, 106
    and themes, 105
Selection, recall and, 38
Selective
    attention, 9, 25–26
    exposure, 83–84
    perception, 29
    recall, 41
Selectivity
    in listening, 90–91
    in perception, 8–10
Self-concept, 71–74
    and communication skills, 72
    learning of, 72
    low, 73
"Self-fulfilling prophecy," 73
Semantic memory, 47, 48, 50
Semantic organization, 36
Semantics, 56
Sensation, 24–25, 30
    and perception, 6, 16
Sentences, creation of, 104
Sharpening, 40
Short-term memory (STM), 33–34, 41
    compared with LTM, 37
Signal
    alteration, 35
    intensity, 16
Signals, 25, 30
    to the brain, 16
Speaking, 99–109
    rate of, 101
Speech, 55
    errors in, 101
    monitoring of, 100
    natural, 101–103
    planning of, 100
    recognition, 91–92

Speech (continued)
   spontaneous, 99–100
Speech processor, innate, 93
Structuring, of information, 18
Superordinate/subordinate
   classification, 48
Symbolic representation, 51
Syntax, 56

Temporal lobe, 14–15
Thalamus, 26n
Themes, and schemata, 105

Timing, and effectiveness of balance
   theory, 80

Unit relationship, 79

VAB system, 69–71
Values, 69–70
Verbal associations, 28, 48–49
Verbal communication, 55–57, 59–62
   and the brain, 15
Visible light spectrum, 16
Vision. *See* Ears and eyes
Vocabulary, 101–102